T0348813

Also by Gary Greenberg

The Pop-Up Book of Phobias
The Pop-Up Book of Nightmares
Self-Helpless (with Jonathan Bines)

BE PREPARED

A PRACTICAL HANDBOOK FOR NEW DADS

20TH ANNIVERSARY EDITION

GARY GREENBERG AND JEANNIE HAYDEN

SIMON & SCHUSTER PAPERBACKS

New York   Amsterdam/Antwerp   London
Toronto   Sydney/Melbourne   New Delhi

Simon & Schuster Paperbacks
An Imprint of Simon & Schuster, LLC
1230 Avenue of the Americas
New York, NY 10020

This publication contains the opinions and ideas of its authors. It is
intended to provide helpful and informative material on the subjects
addressed in the publication. It is sold with the understanding that the
authors and publisher are not engaged in rendering medical, health, or any
other kind of personal professional services in the book. The reader should
consult his or her medical, health, or other competent professional before
adopting any of the suggestions in this book or drawing inferences from it.

The authors and publisher specifically disclaim all responsibility for any
liability, loss, or risk, personal or otherwise, which is incurred as a
consequence, directly or indirectly, of the use and application of any of
the contents of this book.

Copyright © 2004, 2025 by Gary Greenberg and Jeannie Hayden

All rights reserved, including the right to reproduce this
book or portions thereof in any form whatsoever. For information, address
Simon & Schuster Subsidiary Rights Department,
1230 Avenue of the Americas, New York, NY 10020.

This Simon & Schuster trade paperback edition May 2025

SIMON & SCHUSTER PAPERBACKS and colophon are
registered trademarks of Simon & Schuster, LLC.

For information about special discounts for bulk purchases,
please contact Simon & Schuster Special Sales at 1-866-506-1949
or business@simonandschuster.com.

The Simon & Schuster Speakers Bureau can bring authors
to your live event. For more information or to book an event,
contact the Simon & Schuster Speakers Bureau at 1-866-248-3049 or visit
our website at www.simonspeakers.com.

Manufactured in the United States of America

10   9   8   7   6   5   4   3   2   1

Library of Congress Cataloging-in-Publication Data
has been applied for.

ISBN 978-1-6680-6757-4
ISBN 978-1-4391-0332-6 (ebook)

This book is lovingly dedicated to our extraordinary parents,
Marlene and Neil Greenberg and Mary and George Hayden.
They did a wonderful job birthing us, raising us,
and babyproofing the stairs.

CONTENTS

INTRODUCTION

Congratulations, and welcome to the brotherhood of fatherhood.

For thousands of years, dads have roamed the earth, hunting, gathering, trudging through the fields day after day to help provide for their families. But it wasn't until the last half a century that men took a much more active role in the day-to-day duties of raising a child. So if women seem more closely associated with baby care, it's only because they've had a huge head start.

The truth is that men have developed a skill set perfectly suited to new fatherhood. Patience, problem-solving, stamina, and on-the-spot improvisation play a major role in both stalking prey and baby-raising. And much like a beast of the wild, a baby is a very unpredictable creature, prone to sudden mood swings and cranky tirades.

But raw skills alone don't make a great dad. Being prepared is the key—knowing how to handle every possible SNABU (Situation Normal All Babied Up) that can arise in a given day, and being able to implement plans B and C when plan A falls flat. A prepared dad can venture out into the world with the wind in his face and the baby strapped to his back, confident in the knowledge that he is ready for anything. The goal of this book is to foster that confidence.

Of course, *Be Prepared* is not the world's only resource for new fathers. But we like to think it's the most well-researched, concise, and entertaining dad book on the market. Half a million readers can't be wrong. And in this updated 20th anniversary edition, we've delved even deeper to include the very latest research, tips, tricks, and tactics for successful baby-rearing. And if some of the suggestions seem a bit strange at first, rest assured that the book has been vetted by a distinguished member of the American Academy of Pediatrics, Dr. Rebekah Diamond, a board-certified pediatrician and assistant professor at Columbia University.

And since you can't be a good dad without also being a support-ive partner, *Be Prepared* provides insights to all the physical and emotional changes your mate may be experiencing, as well as tips on teamwork, stress management, bartering, and ways to keep the spark alive while you're both covered in spit-up.

At its heart, *Be Prepared* is a how-to manual. It's not the kind of book that waxes emotional about the father-baby relationship. And although we freely admit that sharing your tot's first year is one of the most exciting, life-affirming experiences you'll ever have, we also know that you've got a lot to learn in a short amount of time. So we'll stick to the nuts and bolts and leave the sentiment to you.

Now hoist up your diaper bag and get moving.

Authors' Note

You'll notice that we alternately refer to the baby as "he" and "she" in successive chapters. We decided this would be a good way to make the book feel relatable to all new parents.

THE FIRST WEEK

What Your Newborn WON'T Look Like

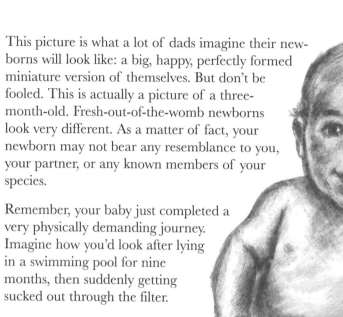

This picture is what a lot of dads imagine their newborns will look like: a big, happy, perfectly formed miniature version of themselves. But don't be fooled. This is actually a picture of a three-month-old. Fresh-out-of-the-womb newborns look very different. As a matter of fact, your newborn may not bear any resemblance to you, your partner, or any known members of your species.

Remember, your baby just completed a very physically demanding journey. Imagine how you'd look after lying in a swimming pool for nine months, then suddenly getting sucked out through the filter.

To familiarize yourself with a newborn's physical appearance, carefully study the picture on page 9. That way you won't be in for any surprises come delivery day. And since you'll get a good view of the baby as she's coming out, and your partner will not, she'll probably be taking her cues from the look on your face. The last thing you want to do is freak her out for no reason.

What Your Newborn WILL Look Like

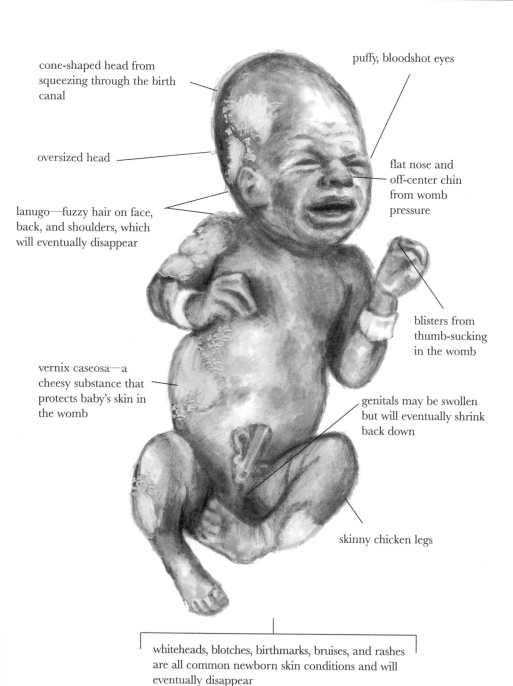

cone-shaped head from squeezing through the birth canal

puffy, bloodshot eyes

oversized head

flat nose and off-center chin from womb pressure

lanugo—fuzzy hair on face, back, and shoulders, which will eventually disappear

blisters from thumb-sucking in the womb

vernix caseosa—a cheesy substance that protects baby's skin in the womb

genitals may be swollen but will eventually shrink back down

skinny chicken legs

whiteheads, blotches, birthmarks, bruises, and rashes are all common newborn skin conditions and will eventually disappear

NEWBORN Party Tricks

REFLEX	confirmed	try again later
	✓	
Rooting		
Moro		
Palmar		
Plantar		
Stepping		
Avoidance		

Let's face it: when you're hanging out with a newborn, you've got to find ways to make your own fun. Conducting a field test of his reflexes is a perfect way to do just that. You'll come away with a greater appreciation of his skills, and you'll have some cool party tricks to pull out at the next family gathering.

Though he looks helpless, your newborn comes pre-programmed with a complete set of reflexes that help him search for and secure food, avoid danger, and extricate himself from sticky situations. Now if you could just get him to apply his own rash cream.

Here are some of the more common reflexes and ways to test for them.

Rooting Reflex

Stimulus: Stroke the baby's cheek.

Response: He will turn his head toward the sensation.

Explanation: This helps the baby find the breast or bottle.

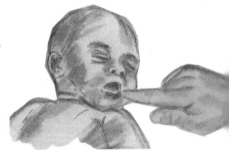

Moro Reflex

Stimulus: Give your baby the slight sensation of falling or make a sudden loud noise.

Response: He'll throw his arms and legs out.

Explanation: This helps him gain his balance or signal for help.

Palmar (Hand) and Plantar (Foot) Grasp Reflexes

Stimulus: Stroke the palm of the baby's hand and the bottom of his foot.

Response: The baby will grasp your finger with his hand, and will curl his toes down toward your finger.

Explanation: This helps baby to reach and grasp objects with his hands. The plantar reflex is an evolutionary holdover from the days when we had to hold on to our mother's fur.

Newborns have such a strong grip that they can hang from a bar, but don't try this at your local gym.

Stepping Reflex

Stimulus: Holding the baby under both arms, stand him up (supporting his head with your fingers) and place his feet on a flat surface.

Response: He'll lift one leg and then the other, simulating a march.

Explanation: This is either a precursor to walking or a way for him to kick objects away.

Avoidance Reflex

Stimulus: With baby lying down, move an object toward his face.

Response: Baby will turn his head from side to side, close his eyes, and try to get out of the way.

Explanation: Self-defense. (Prepares him for dodgeball.)

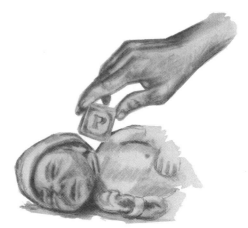

Most reflexes disappear after several months, either evolving into a conscious act or going away completely.

Handing Over the GOODS

VISITORS MUST -WASH HANDS- Before Touching Newborn

Upon seeing the new bundle of joy, your friends and family members will likely fall into two categories: the smotherers and the deserters. The smotherers will engulf the baby with affection, and the deserters will make a beeline for the farthest corner of the room.

Provided they're healthy, it's a good idea to let select loved ones hold the little sprout. You'll get a few moments of freedom, and you can secretly audition potential babysitters in the process.

Moreover, holding a newborn is a rite of passage that brings these people closer to you. It's part of the circle of life. That being said, discourage them from raising up the baby Simba-style.

Before you hand over the baby, here are some things to keep in mind:

- Ask them to wash their hands. A newborn's immune system is not nearly as developed as ours, and viruses are transferred through physical contact. So if you're not careful, you may find yourself standing in the shower at three a.m. trying to decongest his sinuses. Also, feel free to slap a mask on anyone you're even slightly worried about.

- Tell them to relax. Babies, like wild animals, have the ability to pick up on nerves, so the less tense the holder is, the better chance the baby will feel comfortable.

- If you or the receiver are at all uneasy, have them sit down and cross their arms above their lap (see below), and gently place the baby in the crook of their arm. Make sure they support the head. This position is particularly good for children.

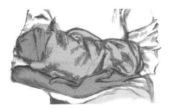

Denying Access

There will be those who ask to hold the baby, and you, for whatever reason, may not feel comfortable letting them. It might be the look in their eyes, the liquor on their breath, the polyester of their jump-suit, or the vape pen dangling from their lips. This is one place where you should definitely trust your instincts, and you can use the handy excuses below to stop them dead in their tracks:

> **"The pediatrician warned us that his rash is very contagious."**
>
> **"The baby is allergic to hair gel/detergent/Axe body spray."**
>
> **"He just got his shots and is very irritable."**
>
> **"He is afraid of people with beards/glasses/face tattoos."**
>
> **"Just warning you they found bedbugs in the hospital nursery."**
>
> **"He has projectile diarrhea, and I don't want to pay your dry-cleaning bill."**

If they don't take these hints, send them on a very important mission to get some random baby product that you need "right away."

BABY BLIMP HEAD

For the first three or four months, everyone who holds your imp will need to support his head and neck area. This is because babies' neck muscles are weak, and their heads are GIGANTIC in relation to the rest of their body.

How gigantic, you ask? A baby's colossal melon measures a whopping one-quarter of their body size. Compare that to an average adult's head, which only measures one-eighth of their body size, and you quickly realize that babies are structurally unsound. Their Easter Island noggins need to be massive to accommodate their ever-expanding brains, which will double in size over the first year.

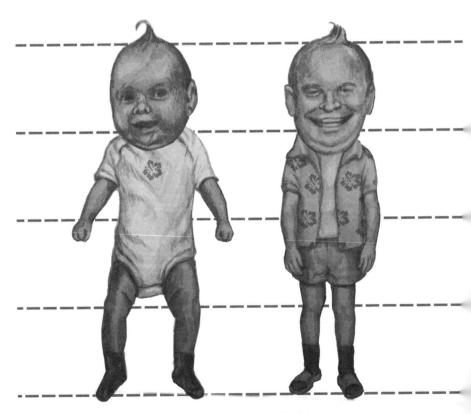

If adults were proportioned like babies, we would look insane.

Baby Cobra

This exercise, commonly referred to as "Tummy Time" (a phrase we promise to never use again), is designed to strengthen your baby's neck and upper-body muscles in order to support that wrecking ball of a head. Simply lay your cherub on his stomach, and he will naturally try to lift his head. You can start off doing this a few times a day for a few minutes at a time, and gradually build from there.

To introduce the Baby Cobra, have your baby lying on top of your bare chest, so he can see your face as you cheer him on. "Buddy, you got this!"

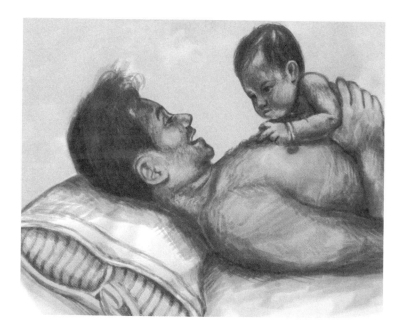

Skins

As a dad, you've got a little catching up to do. The baby has been inside your partner's body for the past nine months. Now it's time for you to bond with him. And there is no better way to connect with a newborn than with skin-to-skin contact. Having him lie on your chest has a bunch of physiological benefits. Most notably, it triggers a powerful hormone called oxytocin to be released in both of you. Oxytocin enhances feelings of well-being and decreases stress. And it's much cheaper than a weed gummy.

Why Your Partner May Not Be
FUNCTIONING PROPERLY

When she's not taking care of the baby, your partner may spend much of the first few weeks collapsed on the couch, your bed, the floor, in the tub—basically, any place that can provide momentary relief. She may not wash her hair, brush her teeth, or change clothes for days on end,

excessive sweating

dizziness

loss of appetite

acne

hot flashes

hair loss

broken eye capillaries from pushing

breast soreness

engorgement

cracked nipples if breastfeeding

abdomen cramping

hand numbness

hand tingling

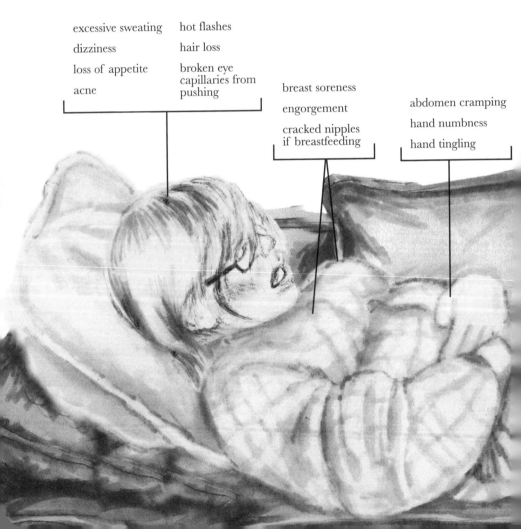

rifling through your closet to find your baggiest shirts and sweatpants. This is all absolutely natural, and necessary. She needs this time to recover from the level-5 tornado that touched down inside her body just days ago.

But have no fear. If the healing goes smoothly, she'll be feeling better, shedding those sweats, and resuming personal hygiene by around three weeks A.B. (after birth).

Below you'll find some of the more common delivery-related afflictions.

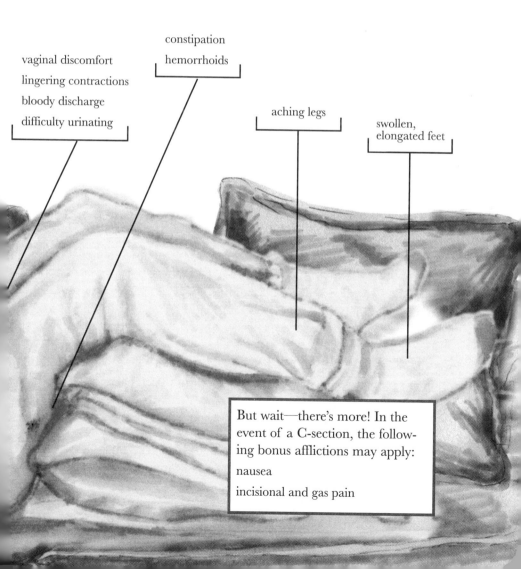

constipation
hemorrhoids

vaginal discomfort
lingering contractions
bloody discharge
difficulty urinating

aching legs

swollen,
elongated feet

But wait—there's more! In the event of a C-section, the following bonus afflictions may apply:

nausea

incisional and gas pain

BREAST VS. BOTTLE

Should you feed your tyke breast milk or formula? This age-old question may be best examined through a head-to-head, topic-by-topic, no-holds-barred comparison.

Nutrition

Winner: Breast milk

As a nutritional product, breast milk is without equal. Not only does it contain antibodies that protect against disease and allergies (as well as containing other valuable enzymes), it actually adapts to the baby's nutritional needs as he grows. It's almost spooky.

Convenience

Winner: Breast milk

Breast milk is the ultimate fast food. It's pre-packaged, preheated, and best of all, nobody can screw up your order.

Cost

Winner (by knockout): Breast milk

Unless your partner is charging by the ounce, breast milk takes this one easily (even if you take into account bottle and pumping supplies).

Smell

Winner: Breast milk

Compared to formula-fed babies, the diapers of breastfed babies don't have much of a smell. This is thought to be a biological adaptation to keep away predators. So if you live anywhere near wild dingoes, definitely opt for breastfeeding.

BREASTFEEDING
First Place

Mother's Birth Recovery

Winner: Breast milk

Nursing helps her uterus shrink back to its original size, and promotes the shedding of excess pregnancy weight.

The Environment

Winner: Breast milk

Producing formula requires land and feed for cattle, fuel for transportation and processing, and plastic and metal packaging. Your partner's milk, on the other hand, is locally sourced, renewable, and comes in its own very elegant, reusable packaging.

Mother's Stress Level

Winner: Formula

Breastfeeding moms have a lot to deal with—pain from feedings and milk production, exhaustion from grabbing sleep in two-hour blocks, and constant worries about the baby getting enough to eat. It can take a big toll on her, and, by extension, you. Formula feeding (or a combo of breast and formula) gives her much more independence, and dads get to take on a larger role in the process.

Results:

Breast 6, Formula 1

Conclusion: If your partner is able to breastfeed, it's a good idea to do so. But if she cannot, don't worry. Almost everyone born in the 1950s through the 1970s was formula-fed, and now these people are running our country! On second thought, you should do whatever you possibly can to breastfeed.

Bidding Farewell to the BREAST

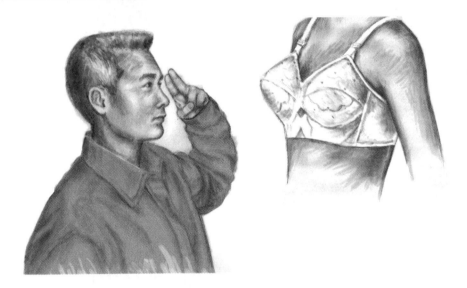

Congratulations, you've just been enrolled in a time-share! But like most time-shares, there is a catch. For the next 4–6 weeks, your voraciously hungry offspring will have sole access to your partner's breasts 24/7. With any luck, your turn will come at some point during month two. Meanwhile, just go about your business and disregard the parade of mammaries flouncing by your face day and night. And don't even consider the irony that at the very moment they become forbidden, her breasts are bigger and firmer than they've ever been before.

Watching your partner breastfeed can trigger a double jealousy. You're jealous of the little milk monster for his all-access pass to your partner's body, and you're jealous of your partner because she can instantly soothe and feed him, while you've got to jump through hoops to quiet him down.

But just because your pecs don't produce a beverage doesn't mean you're off the hook on the breastfeeding front. Studies show that a father's help and support is a key factor in how long and effectively a mother breastfeeds.

Experts recommend breastfeeding for at least six months, followed by a combination of breast milk and solid foods.

Be prepared to chip in by sterilizing and assembling breast pump parts, running for hot compresses in the event of a clogged duct, and presiding over night feedings so that your partner can remain in bed, semiconscious throughout. She will certainly appreciate the effort, and it may help you in expediting that time-share (blackout dates may apply).

To Take Charge of Night Feedings

- bring the baby to the breast
- help him latch on (think of him as the Starship *Enterprise* docking at a space station)
- usher him from one breast to the other (if he is still hungry)
- burp him
- change him
- put him back to sleep

To help your partner maintain milk supply and prevent engorgement, the baby should be feeding from both breasts equally. So if he's just fed from one breast, place a sticky note on the other side of the headboard to remind yourself which side is next.

And after he's been breastfeeding for a month or so, you can take on an even greater role in the baby's dining experience by feeding him his first bottle. This is a profoundly enjoyable experience, followed by an even more delightful moment, his first bottle burp. Bottle burps are usually fuller and deeper than breast burps (on account of the air bubbles). If you want to get this on tape, make sure the mic is close to his mouth so you can catch the full rumble. (For more about bottle-feeding, see page 69.)

You, the night watchman

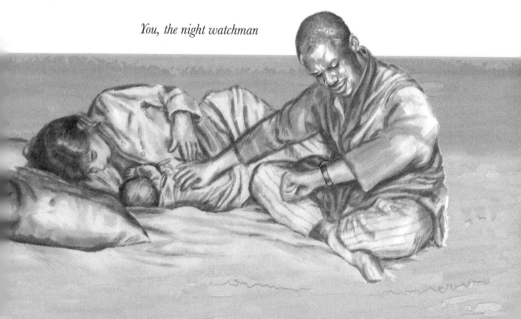

The Call of the Wild

Burping a baby is the perfect task for a dad because, unlike most early baby care, it is results-oriented. You perform a specific series of maneuvers and almost always get a payoff. And when you hear that magical eruption, you can't help but think, "He's one of mine."

Below are three common methods of burping, each one designed for the baby to spit up on a different part of your clothing. This is why you need a burp cloth, or in some cases, a burp tarp. You're in the splash zone, so give yourself as much coverage as possible.

Method A

The baby's head is resting on your shoulder, and your arm is under his bottom. Use your other hand to firmly but gently rub or pat his back.

Method B

Sit him on your lap facing out. Lean him slightly forward as you hold his chest and chin in one hand and rub or pat his back with the other. Be sure to support his head.

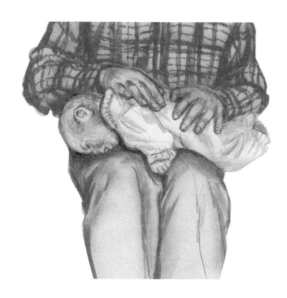

Method C

Lay the baby face down across your lap with his head resting on one knee. Hold his bottom with one hand and rub or pat with the other.

Once your little goober can support his own head, use the following technique to get out the really stubborn gas bubbles. Sit him on your lap, hold him with both hands, and roll his body slowly from side to side and around and around before burping. This can help the air bubbles rise to the surface and reduce the amount of spit-up. Make sure not to tilt him too far to one side or the other.

How often you burp is baby-dependent, but many parents choose to do it twice during a feeding: mid-meal and post-meal. The mid-meal burp will give him room for the second course, like your dad at Thanksgiving.

A Change
Would Do You Good

Since you'll be changing more than 2,500 diapers over the next year, it's worth learning proper technique. Sloppy procedure can result in leakage, rash, or contamination of your clothes and the surrounding area.

For insurance, place a clean diaper under the soiled one.

Place a finger between baby's ankles to keep them from rubbing together.

Procedure

1. Lift the baby's legs off the table using the ankle hold (thumb around one leg, forefinger between the legs, and the rest of your fingers around the other leg).

2. Place a clean diaper under the dirty one, just in case the kid decides to let loose mid-change.

3. Unfasten the tabs of the dirty diaper and stick them back onto themselves, as you don't want them to stick to baby.

4. Lift the butt and remove the diaper, revealing the clean one underneath. For boys, immediately put a washcloth over the crotch. The cold air on their genitals can trigger spontaneous urination.

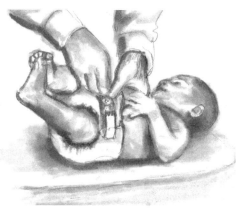

Make sure the diaper is not too tight.

5. Wipe the baby thoroughly. For girls, wipe front to back, to prevent vaginal infection.

6. Fold the bottom of the new diaper up between baby's legs and fasten both sides using the tabs. If you can't fit two fingers between baby's skin and the diaper, then it's too tight.

This method is for disposable diapers. If you are using cloth diapers, the procedure will vary a bit, depending upon the type.

iPoop

During your first-week visit to the pediatrician, they will typically ask about the frequency of feedings, pees, and poops. Some parents keep a legal pad with dates, times, and descriptions of diaper contents. Others use apps. But we found that taking a simple picture on your phone can do the trick, since there is an automatic date and time stamp on each photo. And you'll be able to provide photographic evidence should the doc have any questions.

And won't it be fun, a year from now, when these grisly images show up in your phone's auto-generated "Memories" album?

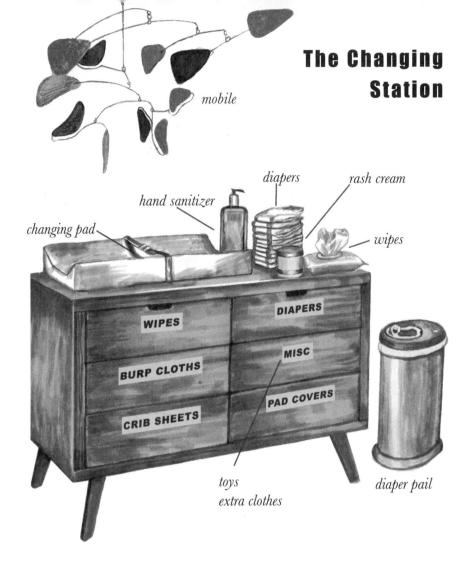

mobile

diapers

rash cream

hand sanitizer

changing pad

wipes

WIPES

DIAPERS

BURP CLOTHS

MISC

CRIB SHEETS

PAD COVERS

toys
extra clothes

diaper pail

Think of yourself as a one-man pit crew. You need to be organized, precise, focused, and adaptable. And although speed is not always imperative, if you wait too long, you may end up with a changing table blowout, which could set you back an hour.

The image above shows a basic setup. You don't need to purchase a dedicated changing table. Instead, put your changing pad on any flat surface, as long as its secure and you have all of your supplies within reach. Dads have retrofitted everything from dressers to desks to mechanic's toolboxes to pool tables (just make sure to put plenty of plastic down first).

Never leave the baby unattended on the changing table.

Diaper Decisions

Environmentally conscious parents have an important choice to make: cloth or disposable diapers?

Approximately 95% of households in the U.S. use disposables. For many first-time parents, sustainability goes out the window when trying to grapple with a brand-new baby. Adding another layer of difficulty (more laundry!), as well as added time and energy, often becomes a nonstarter.

Yet disposable diapers are a huge contributor to plastic waste and landfills. Many of these diapers contain petroleum (a nonrenewable fossil fuel), which breaks down very slowly. So should you feel guilty about using disposables?

Much of the available research concludes that, overall, cloth is more environmentally friendly (and in the long run, cheaper) than disposables. But the question is more nuanced than it seems. Washing cloth diapers at 140°F (necessary for sanitizing them), using a tumble dryer, a diaper service, or partially filling the machine (instead of filling it completely) will actually negate some of their positive environmental impact.

To make things even more confusing, there are many other factors at play, including type of laundry soap, how efficient your machine is, line vs. machine drying, the kind of disposable diaper (some are biodegradable or compostable), whether you use diaper liners, and how your home is powered, to name just a few. We encourage you to do your own research.

Come On, Ride the Train

If you have a network of family and friends who like to cook and seem oddly motivated to see your baby (think *Wheel of Fortune* watchers), strongly consider setting up a meal train so they can help take care of you while you are taking care of the newborn. Since sign-up lists are generally posted online, organizing a meal train can be a perfect job for a tech-savvy sibling or best friend.

Give the organizer the names and emails of everyone in your inner circle. Those who sign up can see available dates and times, any allergies/aversions, and can specify what they're bringing so there is no overlap. Add a few favorite restaurants, too, as some non-cooks may opt for takeout or even food-delivery gift cards. Time it to begin as soon as you arrive home from the hospital (or, if parents are visiting, time it for after they leave and you are—gulp—alone).

A meal train will allow you to spend precious time bonding with your newborn and looking after your partner during those exhausting early days. Think of it as a win-win. You get a fridge full of food, and the giver gets a glimpse of a fresh baby. (But no pressure to entertain. It is common to leave a cooler outside the house.)

Warning: The last day of the meal train can be one of the darker days of early parenthood. But it gives way to another rite of passage: driving around in a fog returning casserole dishes.

Your Newborn
and
Your PET

Dogs

Your dog sees the world a bit differently than you do. To him, you are the alpha male, your partner is the alpha female, and the three of you are a pack. Upon arrival of the baby, the pooch may experience several weeks of postpartum depression. But if all goes smoothly, your new baby will soon be accepted as a junior alpha, eligible for all the benefits of membership—protection, loyalty, and relentless face-licking.

Before the Baby Arrives

- Dogs learn by association, and you don't want your dog to associate the baby with negative things such as diminished playtime, being kicked out of the bedroom, and the relocation of his food dish. If you are going to implement changes, it's important to do so at least a month before the baby arrives.

- Play a recording of a crying baby to get the dog used to loud, high-pitched screams. Dogs have a keen sense of hearing, and may panic upon first listen, but eventually they'll become desensitized and adjust.

- Some dog experts suggest that before the due date, you "play pre-tend" with a doll to acclimate the dog to the new family dynamic. Doggo watches you change, feed, sing to, and put the doll to sleep. This is certainly an option (albeit a very creepy one). It may be less awkward to ask a friend to bring their baby over for an afternoon.

- Make sure your dog understands the "Down!" "Stay!" and "Drop it!" commands, and if not, do some training. Also, take her to the vet to make sure her shots are up to date and that she's parasite-free, and secure someone to take care of her while you're at the hospital yelling "Don't forget to breathe!"

Postpartum

- Soon after the birth, take a piece of clothing that the baby has worn and bring it to your dog so that she can scent-bond.

- Upon arrival from the hospital, your partner should greet the dog first while you hold the baby. Your partner hasn't been home in a while, and the dog's natural excitement may give way to jumping and roughhousing. When all is calm, let her view the baby from ten feet away while on a leash. Then slowly bring the two closer to one another. If the dog remains calm, allow her to sniff the baby. And always be quick to reward good behavior.

- Don't let the pooch lick the wee one's face for the first few months. The baby's immune system is still immature, and your dog's tongue has been to places you'd rather not think about.

- Even the most gentle dogs shouldn't be left alone with the baby.

If all goes well, your baby and your dog will become inseparable.

Cats

Almost all of the dog-based suggestions will work with cats, although you might not have much luck with the commands. Because cats are instinctually drawn to moving objects, they are generally uninterested in newborns. That being said, it's never a good idea to leave the two alone in a room together.

Cats have a tendency to curl up against warm bodies, and may try to get in the crib with your snoring sausage, which is a bad idea, as the cat could inadvertently scratch, bite, or possibly even smother the baby.

Two ways to keep cats out:

- Don't put the crib near a tall bookshelf or bureau. Your parkour-loving pet may leap up to the highest point and then try to launch himself down into the crib.

- After you set up the crib (several months before the due date), stick something on top of the mattress that is really unpleasant for the cat to touch. Cut a piece of cardboard the size of the crib mattress, cover it with double-stick tape, and place it in the crib, so their paws become sticky. Or cover the mattress with tinfoil (they hate the crinkly sound). After one or two ill-fated encounters, they should learn their lesson.

It's not uncommon for cats to exhibit behavioral changes when a newborn arrives. Some will pee on baby items like toys, clothes, or the crib mattress. They may do this to mark their new territory or as a stress response to the household upheaval. To curb this behavior, give them some extra attention, and make sure they have a dedicated space where they can feel safe. And if they still seem anxious, try a pheromone diffuser or feline CBD oil to take the edge off.

A Japanese study from 2022 found that dog ownership was linked to fewer cases of postpartum depression in mothers, whereas cat ownership was linked to an increased number of postpartum cases. (Cat people, please address your angry letters to The Ministry of the Environment, Tokyo, Japan.)

Your Baby and Social Media

Of all the chapters in this field guide to fatherhood, this one carries the most risk of being hopelessly outdated by the time you read it. As technology rapidly evolves, there will be new sites, new ways to post, and new ways for foreign governments to scoop up all of our personal data. For all we know, as you are reading this, AI chatbots are auto-posting your baby's every bowel movement.

We do feel confident one thing won't change:

When your baby finally arrives, you will want to show him off far and wide. But how? Whether you are posting a birth announcement or celebrating his first tooth, social media has made it easier—and more complicated than ever before—to be a proud papa.

To Post or Not to Post?

You might not think that someone who crawls around half naked all day would have privacy issues, but babies absolutely do. Studies have suggested that kids will have well over 1,000 images on social media by the time they are five years old. Meanwhile, a growing number of parents are considering whether to post any images at all before their children can legally consent. Generally, privacy policies of social media sites are even denser than stroller assembly guides, so a good rule of thumb is to assume anything you post will be totally out of your hands.

Of course, posting alone does not make you a reckless dad, but a little caution can go a long way:

- Be careful with whom you share his date of birth and location. Because they are basically blank slates, children are particularly vulnerable to identity theft. About 1 in 50 kids will be affected at some point, with many not finding out until much later.

- Never post pictures of your child in a state of undress—for safety and privacy reasons. Remember, digital footprints last forever. Ten years from now, would he want a bathtub tantrum shot to come up in a name search?

- Even if you don't post the location and date of birth, most photos taken on a phone contain metadata including the date, time, and GPS location of where the picture was taken. Anyone can quickly and easily access this info. (You can download apps that remove metadata.)

- Consider setting your account to private, so that only approved followers can view your posts. Alternatively, you can bypass social media entirely and create a shared album on any phone or tablet. That way, when you accidentally befriend a Russian hacker online, he'll have no idea you're a family man.

- Never share photos of other children without parental permission, and expect others to follow suit. As hard as it is to resist posting adorable group playdates, respect everyone's privacy. (You can always blur their faces, or place graphic privacy stickers over them.)

- If anyone has posted anything that is not okay with you, don't be shy about letting them know.

- Have your relatives get permission from you and your partner before posting any baby pics. This is especially true for newborn hospital shots, where emotions (and sideboob) are at an all-time high.

Become a PAPA-razzi

In general, moms take a million adorable photos of dads and their babies, but for some reason, dads often don't respond in kind. This is why the web is flooded with posts and articles from frustrated moms lamenting this very point. It's your job to break the cycle and snap away!

Snap and Release

Well-intentioned relatives will likely be gifting you a wide array of baby stuff, from clothes to books to old toys and equipment that's been boxed up in their basement for decades. Some of these will be welcome additions to your home. Others you will immediately want to throw into a wood chipper.

Before you cart all of the unwanted items to the nearest donation box, set up a photo session and snap a pic of the baby with each. Even though your precious one looks hideous wearing that purple and brown tie-dyed onesie, and would immediately rip off and swallow the eyeballs of the fifty-year-old windup robot, you'll warm the hearts of your loved ones by sending them photographic evidence of the joy (and possibly tetanus) they've brought your family.

How to Entertain
a NEWBORN

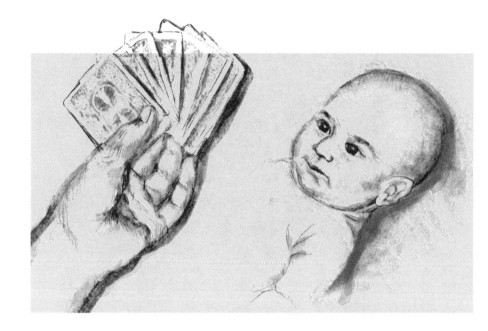

One of the best—and only—ways to interact with your newborn is through stimulus-response games, where you pre-
sent him with various objects or sensations and wait for a
reaction. And yes—staring blankly is considered a reaction.

The following games focus on sensory development.

Vision

Newborns' eyes can focus best on objects 10–12 inches away from
their faces, and they can't see colors.

Clubs and Spades

Grab a deck of cards, separate out the clubs and spades, and hold
them in front of your baby. Slowly fan them out, bring them back
in, and fan them out again. Show him a royal flush and see if his
poker face holds.

Hearing

Your small fry started hearing sounds in the womb—his mother's heartbeat, the air going in and out of her lungs, muffled human voices, and the gurgling of her stomach working on that four a.m. meal of Taco Bell and sour gummy worms.

Sound Tracking

On one side of baby, crinkle a bag, shake a can of nuts, or jingle your keys until baby turns his head to the sound, then do the same on the other side.

Karaoke

Babies are the perfect audience for karaoke, for two reasons: (1) there's evidence that newborns prefer the sound of the human voice to other sounds, and (2) no matter how pitchy you are, they won't be able to crawl away for another six months.

Touch

Touch is the first sense to develop in the womb, and by birth it is fairly evolved. Some areas are more responsive than others, with the palms of the hands, the bottoms of the feet, and the area around the mouth being the most sensitive.

The Texture Buffet

Gently rub different areas of your baby's skin with objects of varying textures. Suggestions include a clean damp sponge, a silk tie, the fur lining of a glove, and a bicycle pump to blow air on him.

Smell

Newborns have a keen sense of smell, and within the first couple of days show a distinct preference for the scent of their mother's milk.

Fridge Inventory

Take a bunch of odiferous foods out of the fridge—cheese, onions, pickles, and fish are good choices—and hold them up to your newborn's nose. Wait for a reaction. If you aren't sure if the yogurt has gone bad, perhaps his face will give you the answer.

Taste

Your tadpole's taste buds began developing in utero, and he will now show a distinct preference for sweet tastes rather than sour ones. But seeing as babies can't have anything but breast milk or formula for around six months, you'll have to curb your impulse to have him suck on a lemon wedge.

THE FACIAL RECOGNITION TEST

Show the baby the four faces on these pages. See how he gravitates toward the recognizable face? This preference is genetically built in and helps newborns bond with their parents. And if by chance your baby prefers one of the other faces, you just may have a budding Picasso on your hands.

0–3 MONTHS

The First Month Slump

Fatherhood can hit you like a sucker punch. The baby arrives, and friends and family shower you with gifts, help, and food for a few weeks. Then suddenly it's a ghost town. And you are struck by this overwhelming feeling that nothing will ever be the same again. Someone has taken away your old life and replaced it with this long, frustrating community service project.

You may feel anxious, depressed, and lonely. And why shouldn't you? You're completely at the mercy of a relentless little dictator, and there is no relief in sight. But as you're wallowing, it's important to remember that you are not alone. Fathers the world over, from Copenhagen to Cape Town, from presidents to porta-potty scrubbers, have all gone through this rough patch.

For the majority of dads, this phase lasts somewhere between eight and twelve weeks, at which point you switch into the "I might as well make the best of it" phase. Several factors combine to help lift the dark clouds from your head, including:

- The baby is sleeping longer hours.

- You're feeling more adept at handling and troubleshooting her.

- She's finally smiling at you (the baby, not your partner).

If you start to feel defeated or withdrawn, talk to your partner and friends and consider seeking professional help. Male postpartum depression is not often talked about, but studies have shown that roughly one in ten new dads suffers from PPD.

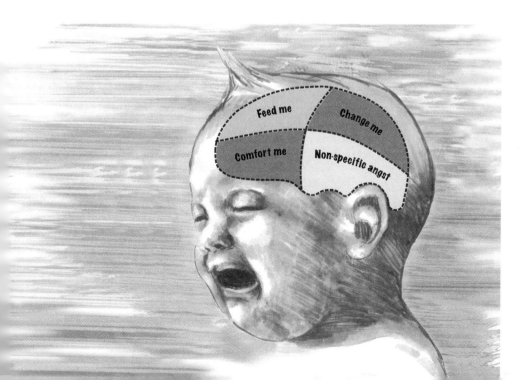

Moms and Mood Swings

Not to be confused with PMS, PPMS (Postpartum Mood Swings) affects almost all new moms in one way or another. This condition is often referred to as the Baby Blues, but the word "blues" does not do it justice.

Plainly speaking, your partner may be all over the map, so expect the unexpected. One minute she'll scream at you for leaving a diaper on the floor, and another she'll weep uncontrollably because you ate the last toaster strudel without consulting her first. She may banish you to the basement (even if you don't have one!), then criticize you for not being romantic. Try to think of it as your penance for not having gone through labor.

Keep in mind that much of this behavior is just nature taking its course. Right after pregnancy, her estrogen and progesterone levels decrease significantly, causing mood swings, irritability, and anxiety. So if you see her throwing breast pump parts across the living room, remember to cut her some slack . . . and duck.

PPMS can last anywhere from a couple of days to a month or more. It can really take a toll on you, as you are already trying to adjust to the new baby. But since getting a room at the Best Western is not an option, you've got to do everything you can to help her through this rough patch.

Four Policies to Help Ensure Your Survival (and Hers)

Policy #1 Ears Open, Mouth Closed
Men tend to be fixers by nature. You see a problem, and you find the solution. But in this case, your partner may need comfort, reassurance, and praise, not a PowerPoint presentation.

Policy #2 Strike It from the Record
Try to remember all the unhinged things that you've said after a night of drinking. Now consider that she's under the influence of chemicals far more mind-altering than Jose Cuervo. So just nod, apologize, and don't try to win the argument. Six months from now, she may not even remember some of the names she called you. (You should write them down, though just in case.)

Policy #3 Be an Army of One
Don't expect too much from your partner these first weeks. You may need to do everything short of breastfeeding, so be prepared to carry the load. And if you ever start to feel put-upon, stifle it and be grateful you weren't the one who had a baby inside you, speed-bagging your bladder like Mike Tyson. Enlist the help of friends and relatives and order plenty of takeout, or set up a meal train. (See meal train section on page 28.)

Policy #4 Take Her Out
Isolation is a big contributor to PPMS, so the sooner she gets a change of scenery, the quicker she may come around. Remember that newborns are very portable, so grab her and the bambina and take a stroll around the block. The exercise will help her get her strength back, and it releases endorphins, which can lighten her mood.

Postpartum Depression

This condition is far more serious than PPMS, and affects between 10 and 20% of new moms. If your partner's emotional state is seriously impeding her ability to function, or her symptoms last longer than a month, suggest that she consult her obstetrician. There are also plenty of good resources online, including Postpartum Support International. If she resists getting help, you can bring up the fact that her condition is very treatable, and that every day she waits is one less day she'll be able to enjoy the tot.

Tub Time

Bathing a baby is a mission that requires a steady hand and nerves of steel, which is why it's a perfect challenge for a new dad.

For a segment of the population that just lounges around all day, newborns get surprisingly dirty. Without regular cleanings, that fresh new baby scent can quickly give way to the odor of spoiled milk. Bathe her every few days, or as much as seems necessary, but if her skin starts to dry out, you'll have to cut back.

Don't give a bath until the umbilical stump and (if you've got a circumcised boy) the circumcision scar have healed. Before then, conduct a simple sponge down.

Bathing Equipment Checklist

- ☐ A baby tub or other bathing apparatus
- ☐ A large plastic bucket
- ☐ A plastic cup
- ☐ Baby soap and shampoo
- ☐ Two or three washcloths
- ☐ A dry towel next to the tub in which to wrap baby upon completion

Wash 'n' Where?

When deciding where to bathe your little one, take into consideration safety, your comfort, her comfort, and proximity to a water source.

Options include:

In a Baby Tub Placed in the Sink

Many tubs dock right into the sink bay, anchoring it into place. Also, having the baby at this height will give you good leverage, and you'll be right next to a water source. Just make sure that you point the faucet away from her at all times.

On the Floor

Nervous parents sometimes place the tub on the floor for the first couple of baths, until they feel confident that they won't drop the wigglepuss. Make sure you tarp the floor under the staging area, and use a pillow under your knees.

In a Baby Tub Inside the Big Tub

This can be a bit hard on the back, but the baby is low to the ground, and it won't matter if water goes everywhere.

With You in the Big Tub

Some babies find the little tub confining, and would prefer your company. The big tub offers both of these options, but it's not recommended until she's around six months old.

Bathing Procedure

1. Pour 3–4 inches of water into the tub and fill the bucket. The water should be nice and warm, but not hot. Test it with your elbow, and if it feels hot to you, then it's definitely too hot for the baby. And if you don't trust your elbow, grab a meat thermometer. The ideal temp is around 100°F.

2. Undress the baby and place her in the tub. To keep her from becoming cold and whiny, lay a washcloth across her chest and keep pouring warm water from the bucket over her. But always have one hand holding her in place.

3. Using a clean washcloth, wipe the eyes from the bridge of the nose out. Then move on to the rest of the face, outer ears, and neck. A baby's neck folds are surprisingly cavernous, providing ample storage space for dirt, lint, fermenting spit-up, and perhaps even spare change. If left unwashed, the folds can become infected and start to smell like curdled yogurt.

4. Move on to the arms, legs, and torso. The armpits, belly button, and leg folds are also perfect nooks for dirt and grime to settle. Use baby soap on the body a few times a week, and just water the rest of the time, but you can soap the diaper area every time. Rinse off the soap with cups of clean water from the bucket.

5. Wash the hair. Because babies lose much of their heat through their heads, do this last. Use a couple of drops of baby shampoo several times a week.

6. Place her on a dry towel and pat her dry

Keeping Shampoo Out of Your Baby's Eyes

To avoid getting shampoo in her eyes, use one of the following tactics:

- Place a dry washcloth over her eyes as you pour water onto her head before and after lathering her up; or

- Swaddle the baby (see page 60). Then hold her over the tub with her back on your forearm, her legs tucked inside your elbow, and her head and neck supported by your wrist and hand. This is called the football hold. Tip her head down so that when you rinse her hair, the soapy water will drip down into the tub and not into her eyes.

Use the football hold to rinse your baby's hair.

Cradle Cap

When you are washing your little one's hair, you may notice big scaly flakes on her scalp. Don't worry, you haven't birthed a Gorgon. This is called cradle cap, a common and harmless newborn condition that doesn't seem to cause any discomfort and usually disappears by about three months, just in time for the daycare prom. If you want to get rid of the scales, you can massage the scalp with mineral oil or petroleum jelly, remembering to be gentle around the fontanels (the soft spots on the top of her head). You can also use a soft toothbrush to clean her scalp. Avoid putting hats on her when indoors, because sweat can exacerbate the condition.

Gripping a Slippery Squirt

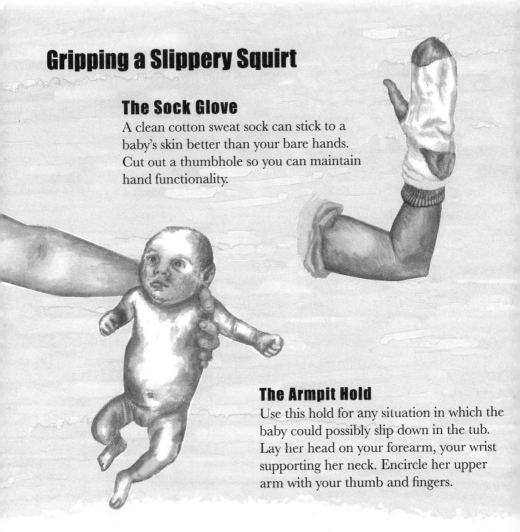

The Sock Glove

A clean cotton sweat sock can stick to a baby's skin better than your bare hands. Cut out a thumbhole so you can maintain hand functionality.

The Armpit Hold

Use this hold for any situation in which the baby could possibly slip down in the tub. Lay her head on your forearm, your wrist supporting her neck. Encircle her upper arm with your thumb and fingers.

The Diving Reflex

At some point or another you may accidentally lose your grip, and the baby's head will go underwater for a second or two. Don't panic. Newborns come equipped with something called the Diving Reflex, an automatic response that prevents them from breathing in water should they go under. In the few seconds it would take you to pull your baby back up, chances are great there would be no harm done to her. This reflex lasts for a few months and then disappears.

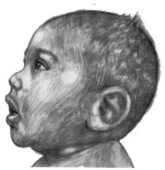

Accidents Will Happen

No matter how many visible warning signs you post, it's almost inevitable that your baby will, at some point, leave you a surprise in the tub. They have an instinct for it, like a squid releasing ink when threatened. While undeniably gross, dealing with a bath bomb is one of those parental rites of passage that marks your official entry into dadhood. Congrats!!!

In order to decontaminate the tub, you'll need to:

- Pull the baby out, wrap her in a towel, and place her on a secure surface.

- Quickly drain the tub, rinse it out with soap and water, and then refill it.

- Get another clean towel for post-bath wrapping, put the baby back in, and start over.

As far as urine in the tub goes, most new dads don't change the water, for these reasons:

- It's really hard to tell if a baby has peed in the tub.

- Urine is mostly water anyway.

- Dads have relieved themselves in the shower for millennia, and their feet have never fallen off.

Who Are You Wearing?

If you don't own a baby carrier, what are you waiting for? You're missing out on one of the most satisfying and convenient ways to hang out with your munchkin.

Benefits for the Baby The rhythm of your heartbeat and your body warmth and movement provide her a feeling of comfort and safety. Carried babies often cry less and sleep better. And being elevated lets her engage more with her surroundings, promoting social development.

Benefits for You Not only is it a great way to soothe and bond with the imp, but having her in the carrier means both of your hands are free, which is a real game changer. Your mindset shifts from "I can't get anything done because of this baby" to "I can do everything with this baby strapped to me!"

You're instantly freed up for yard work, laundry, stretching, baking, walking the dog, running errands, hiking, and grabbing a cup of joe with friends, all with your next of kin proudly mounted to your chest like a hood ornament. You'll notice that random strangers will smile, coo, and, completely ignoring all cues, even flirt with you.

Because there are a few different styles of carriers on the market, there may be some trial and error before you find the make and model that's most comfortable for you and the baby.

Until she can hold her head up unassisted (at around four to six months old), she'll need to be facing you, giving her the perfect opportunity to vomit down your chest.

You may need to adjust your cornhole throwing mechanics.

Coping with Crying

A baby's cry can be as loud as a chainsaw or leaf blower.

If you have the misfortune of working for a tireless, demanding boss, we've got bad news for you: now you've got a pair of them. And the baby is undoubtedly the less forgiving of the two. But then again, you'll never be able to appease your other boss by blowing a raspberry on their stomach.

If you are skeptical about your fussbucket's absolute power over you, try to spend thirty seconds NOT responding to her wails. The sound of a baby's cry has been evolutionarily designed to be incredibly annoying to humans, in order to ensure that we'll drop whatever we're doing and rush over to them. The sound triggers a biological "alarm reaction" that:

- raises your blood pressure,
- increases your circulation, and
- elevates oxygen levels to your brain

So the baby's Pavlov, and you're the dog. And on top of that, the human ear is most sensitive to sounds at 3 kHz, almost the exact central frequency of a baby's cries.

Discomfort
Fatigue
Pain
Hunger
Colic
Boredom

IDENTIFYING THE SIX CRIES

Be prepared to spend approximately 500 hours of your baby's first year listening to her cry, give or take a wail or two. If you'd like to be on the low end of this curve, you'll need to be able to figure out what she needs at any given moment. That's why you should learn how to identify the six baby cries.

Like the British code breakers of World War II, you've got to use your powers of decryption to understand your wee one's seemingly random wails. Listen to her cadence, tone, pitch, and volume. Mark it in your memory, and then respond. Does a bottle quiet her? If so, you've discovered the hungry cry. If not, try one of the many other maneuvers described on the following pages. You'll soon become cry-lingual.

Not every baby cries exactly the same way, but there are six basic patterns that are common among kiddos worldwide.

Hunger

A series of low-pitched, rhythmic moans, growing more and more insistent. Short cry, pause, louder cry, pause, even louder cry. This is sometimes accompanied by putting her fingers in her mouth or smacking her lips.

Fatigue

A soft, breathy blubbering. If you listen closely you may hear vibrato. The cry is often accompanied by eye rubbing.

Pain

A high-pitched cry that comes out of nowhere. It's like somebody triggered a car alarm.

Discomfort

A consistent pattern of forceful sobs, which can break into a full-scale wail if not attended to. Discomfort cries are usually about being too hot or too cold, an uncomfortable body position, or a soiled diaper.

Boredom

A low-volume whimper that stops and starts irregularly. It doesn't sound frantic, but slowly builds in intensity. This cry will usually cease the moment you enter the room.

Colic

A burst of urgent high-pitched screaming that can go on for hours. Each shriek can last four or five seconds. A lengthy pause follows while she catches her breath, then it starts all over again.

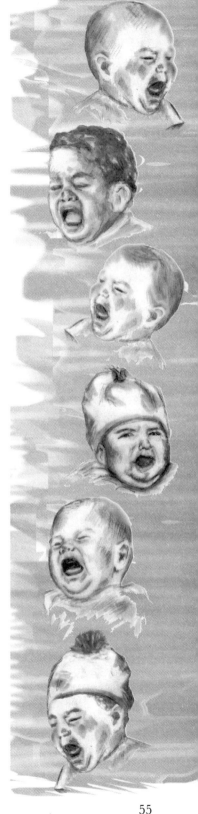

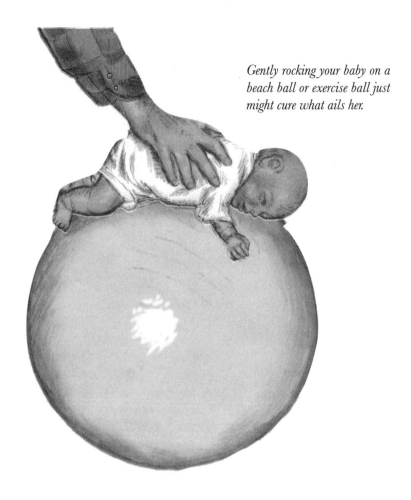

Gently rocking your baby on a beach ball or exercise ball just might cure what ails her.

Hardcore Soothing Tactics

What happens when you've tried all of the obvious soothers and yet she's still sobbing uncontrollably? It's time to break out some alternative tactics. Rest assured the methods below have been proven effective, they just aren't as well-known as the classics. For instance, the baby-on-the-ball idea wasn't discovered until a resourceful dad, whose arms were falling asleep from holding his bawling daughter, decided to rest her on a nearby exercise ball. He began gently rolling the ball around and around, his hand firmly on her back. She miraculously quieted, and lo and behold, a soothing tactic was born.

If one method doesn't work for you, move on to another. But don't cross any of them off your list, because what works today might not work tomorrow, and vice versa.

Gas Relief

Gas bubbles can cause havoc in the newborn digestive system.

- Lay your little weeper on her back and bicycle her legs back and forth, or bring both knees up to her chest and then down and repeat. This pressure on the stomach frequently causes an exciting gas expulsion.

- Sit in a swivel chair. Place the baby face down on your lap, and swing the chair back and forth while gently patting her back.

- Try gripe water or colic drops. These over-the-counter potions are designed to reduce infant gas. (Make sure to use a reputable, trusted brand.)

- If your partner is breastfeeding, you might suggest she avoid some of the gassier foods like beans, cabbage, and broccoli for a few days to see if it helps with fussiness. Tell her that you and the baby will both appreciate it.

Change of Scenery

Giving the scamp a new perspective may calm her down.

- Climbing up and down stairs with her in your arms combines interesting visuals with exciting motion. It's also a great way to work those quads and glutes.

- Put her in the stroller and meander up and down the hallway.

- Hold her in front of a mirror. She may be mesmerized by the sight of the new kid or transfixed by the reflection of your baggy-eyed face behind her.

Startling

If you startle a crying baby, sometimes she will forget why she was crying in the first place. But once the crying stops, be prepared to quickly segue into another activity.

- Turn off the lights, wait a few seconds, and then turn them on again. Repeat if necessary.

- Place her hand or foot under running water (but test the water temp first).

- Imitate the baby's cry right back to her. Use the same tone, pace, and volume, accompanied by a goofy, exaggerated face. She may stop to watch. And as soon as she does, you stop, too.

- Gently blow on your baby's face with a short puff of air. This triggers the Diving Reflex, which makes her hold her breath for a brief moment, and can short-circuit a crying spell.

- Take a deep breath, and then let out a loud, long "Shhhhhhhhh-hhhhh . . ." You may be tempted to add an ". . . iiiiiit" to the end.

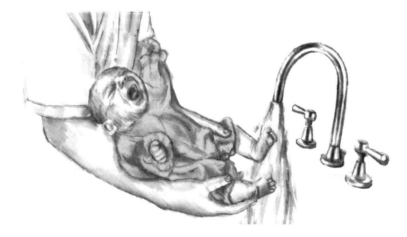

A while back, a few desperate, innovative dads tried gently tossing a slice of American cheese onto their babies' heads, which can sometimes stop a sobbing spree. We can't, in good conscience, recommend this practice, but do yourself a favor and google this internet classic.

Re-creating the Womb

Some babies long for their former residence.

- Dim the lights. The womb is not completely dark, but it doesn't usually get brighter than a dimly lit nightclub.

- Put her in the car-seat carrier, grab the handle, and gently swing her back and forth. This can approximate the closeness and motion she felt in the womb. You can also buy an electronic swing to replicate this motion.

- Many babies suck their fingers in the womb. You can either use a pacifier or let the baby suck on your freshly washed pinkie. Make sure the finger is palm-side up so it doesn't scratch the roof of her mouth.

- A warm bath with white noise in the background can help her regain the feeling of being enveloped.

- Immobilize her with a swaddle . . .

If you are nearing the end of your rope, don't be too proud to pass the baton to your partner. The baby may respond to her new smell, voice, and touch, and you'll get some time to decompress, at least until she returns the favor.

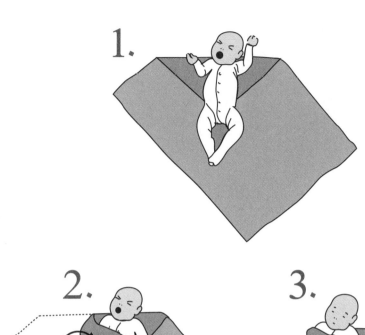

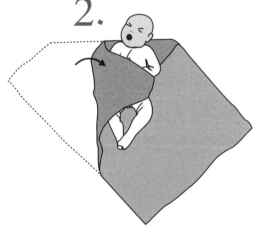

Swaddling

Swaddling mimics the closeness and security of the womb. Though many babies are comforted by this miniature straitjacket, others would rather not revisit the "in utero" experience, thank you, and will quickly tell you so.

Follow the step-by-step instructions below. A square blanket may hold better than a rectangular one, but either can be used.

1. **Place a blanket on a flat surface, and fold one corner down about six to eight inches. Then lay the baby down so her head is directly above the folded corner.**

2. **Take the left corner of the blanket and pull it across her body, tucking it in under her back.**

3. **Fold the bottom of the blanket up to the baby's chest and tuck it into the first fold.**

4. **Grab the right corner and pull it across her body and behind her back.**

5. **If you have enough blanket, you can tuck the right corner into the fold beneath the back of the baby's neck.**

If your baby prefers having her arms free, you can try a modified swaddle by repeating the above steps with both the left and right sides tucked in under her arms. (Once they can roll over, all babies should be swaddled with their arms out.)

You can also buy swaddling alternatives like sleep sacks and wearable blankets, which give the baby a little more wiggle room, and don't require you to learn origami.

Bracing for Unhappy Hour

The sun is setting, so you start to relax and unwind from your busy day and melt into the calm of twilight's warm embrace. And suddenly your bundle of joy transforms into a ball of rage. It's time for Unhappy Hour.

Also known as Witching Hour, presumably because your baby turns into an incubus, Unhappy Hour usually occurs between the hours of five and eight, and is marked by extreme edginess and constant wailing, sometimes lasting for ninety minutes or more. This could be caused by a number of factors, including overstimulation, overtiredness, or just baby being baby.

If you work outside the home, this can be particularly miserable. Just as you open the door, the baby implodes. It could start to give you a complex.

When all of your best soothing efforts go unrewarded, anxiety and frustration may set in, bringing you one step closer to putting that "Bundle of Joy: Gently Used" ad on craigslist.

But here are three facts that might make you feel better:

- Unhappy Hour affects over 75% of all babies, so it's NOT YOUR FAULT.

- This pattern should stop at around twelve weeks.

- Letting the baby cry in her crib for a couple of minutes in between comforting attempts won't traumatize her, and just may be a welcome break for the both of you.

In the meantime, get a pair of earplugs to dampen the noise level, which can reach 100 decibels, about the same level as a chainsaw, leaf blower, or high-end blender. So make yourself a frozen daiquiri and drown out the noise for thirty seconds.

Combating Colic

It strikes suddenly and without warning, wreaks havoc on your household, then vanishes as swiftly as it came, leaving a trail of frazzled nerves and empty aspirin bottles in its wake. It goes by the name of colic, and it might be knocking on your door.

What's the difference between Unhappy Hour and colic? In a general sense, your baby has colic when she cries inconsolably for at least:

three hours a day,
three days a week,
for three weeks.

It's known as the 3-3-3 rule. And if you have twins with colic, that's 6-6-6, the devil's number, and it will feel just like a visit from Beelzebub.

Although colic afflicts up to a quarter of all babies, no one knows exactly what causes it. Many experts think that it's got something to do with digestion. Fortunately, there are tactics to combat the little C. You can try some of the gas-relief suggestions discussed previously, as well as the two additional methods below.

The Popeye Hold

1. Lay the baby face down on one of your forearms, with her head near the crook of your elbow.

2. Place your other hand on her back.

3. Rock her from side to side while stroking her back.

Your forearm is exerting gentle pressure on her abdomen, which, in combination with the rocking, may soothe her.

The Cry and Dry

1. Take a warm towel out of the clothes dryer and put a cool towel in. Turn the dryer on.

2. Hop on the dryer. Fold or roll up the warm towel and place it on your lap. (Make sure it's not too hot.)

3. Lay the baby on her belly across your lap so that her stomach rests directly on top of the towel. Hold her bottom with one hand and stroke her back with the other.

4. When the towel cools down, open the dryer and switch towels. Turn the dryer back on, fold the warm towel, and repeat step 3.

The combination of the heat, vibration, position, noise, and your hands on the baby's back may prove too powerful for even the most stubborn case of colic. The laundry room may become your second home for a while.

Wrestling the Breast Pump

If you have complicated feelings surrounding the breast pump, it's completely understandable. After all, it's a bit unnerving watching a mechanical device mercilessly tugging at your partner's bare chest. You can't help but think, "If robots made pornography, this is what it would look like."

But if you think it's off-putting for you, it's got to be doubly surreal for your partner. She is literally hooked up to the mammary matrix—a gurgling, wheezing, insatiable device that won't stop milking until you shut it down.

But you'll soon realize that the pump is your friend. Not only will it relieve your partner from painful clogging and engorgement, it will also allow you to bottle-feed your baby, one of the most satisfying new-dad activities out there. And having a fridge full of stored breast milk will finally free you both up to get someone to watch her while you go out on an actual date for once.

There are two types of pumps: manual and electric. Manual pumps are inexpensive, lightweight, and small, so your partner can use them at work or in transit. But the constant hand-squeezing can be both tiring and time-consuming.

Most electric pumps are heavier and more cumbersome, but they simply latch on and go to work. They're also rigged for double-barrel pumping. If your partner is trying to increase output, you'll want one with a powerful motor.

Just remember that milk production, like old-school capitalism, is based on supply and demand, so the more milk she pumps, the more she will produce.

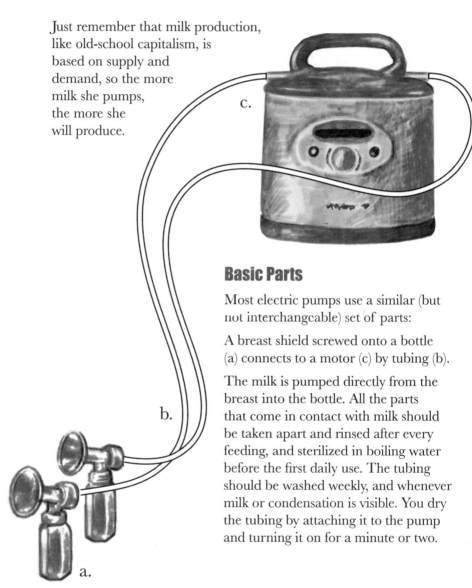

Basic Parts

Most electric pumps use a similar (but not interchangeable) set of parts:

A breast shield screwed onto a bottle (a) connects to a motor (c) by tubing (b).

The milk is pumped directly from the breast into the bottle. All the parts that come in contact with milk should be taken apart and rinsed after every feeding, and sterilized in boiling water before the first daily use. The tubing should be washed weekly, and whenever milk or condensation is visible. You dry the tubing by attaching it to the pump and turning it on for a minute or two.

There are also small wearable electric pumps that slip right into a bra for stealth pumping.

The FDA advises against using a secondhand pump due to contamination risks, so it's best to buy your own or rent one from a hospital.

If your partner has any problems with breastfeeding or pumping, you can contact your local lactation consultant or La Leche League, an international breastfeeding organization.

Storing Pumped Milk

Short-Term Storage Detach the container from the pump, seal it up, write the date on a piece of tape, and stick it to the bottle. Milk can last 4–6 days in the fridge.

Long-Term Storage You can purchase generic disposable bottle bags for easy milk storage. Or, as an alternative, pour the milk into clean, sterile ice cube trays, place the trays in sealed freezer bags, and put them in the freezer. The milk will last 4–6 months. When you are ready to use it, pop an ice cube from the tray, put it in a plastic baggie, and heat it under warm water. When it's liquefied, transfer it to a bottle. Each cube equals approximately two ounces of milk.

Store breast milk in ice cube trays, but be sure to mark them so there won't be any surprises at your next party.

Glossary of Breastfeeding Terms
That You Might As Well Know

Colostrum Thick yellowish liquid secreted from the breasts during the first days postpartum, before the breast milk comes in. Colostrum provides the baby with vital nutrients and antibodies.

Engorgement Common during the first weeks of breastfeeding, engorgement occurs when breasts are filled to capacity, often causing discomfort. Remedies include immediate feeding, pumping, and warm compresses.

Clogging When a milk duct is blocked, a tender lump appears on the breast, and it may be painful. Remedies include emptying the breast regularly, massages, and warm compresses.

Rooting Reflex A newborn's instinct to turn her head toward any stimulus that brushes her cheek. She may also open her mouth, stick her tongue out, and search for a nipple.

Nipple Confusion No, it's not a band performing at Coachella. Nipple confusion refers to babies who have a hard time switching between breastfeeding and bottle-feeding.

The Boppy Pillow An unfortunately named horseshoe-shaped cushion that fits around the torso to support the baby's body during feedings. Later on, as the baby tries to sit up, you can put the pillow around her so she won't "bop" her head on the floor. It also becomes an entertaining headpiece.

The evolution of the Boppy Pillow

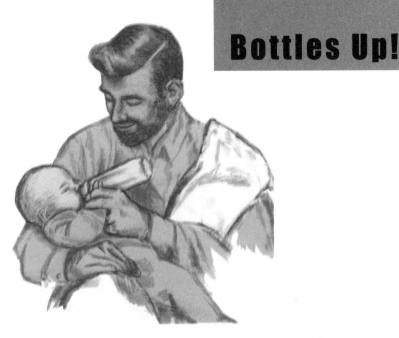

Bottles Up!

Giving your little goober a bottle is your initiation into Total Provider status. It's comforting to know that if your partner were ever glitched into a parallel universe, you could still feed the baby until she reappeared.

And once the baby accepts the bottle from you, she'll most likely accept it from others, which means you and your partner will finally be able to hire a babysitter, drive to a romantic overlook, and sleep in the car.

Bottle-feeding tips:

- If your partner is nursing, introduce the bottle when the baby is around one month old. Any earlier and she may still be figuring out the breast; any later and she may be too set in her nursing ways.

- Don't be discouraged if she doesn't take to it immediately. Keep trying with different nipple shapes and sizes, and with milk at various temperatures. Almost all babies eventually catch on.

- Limit bottle-feeding to a few times a day. You don't want her to reject the breast.

- Administer these first feedings without your partner in the room. The baby may look at her and get confused. And your partner may start sobbing, seeing the bottle as an early symbol that your little one is leaving the nest.

Bottle-Feeding Step-By-Step

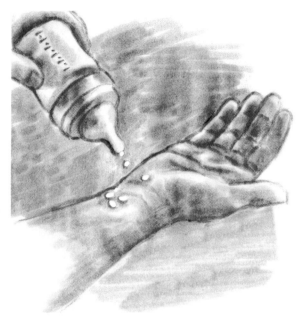

1. Warm Although it's not absolutely necessary, many folks warm up the bottle to get it closer to the temperature of breast milk. To do so, run the bottle under hot water or buy a bottle warmer. Never use a microwave, because it destroys enzymes, and the milk heats unevenly.

2. Test Temperature Squirt a few milk droplets onto the underside of your wrist. The bottle should be no hotter than body temperature.

3. Bait the Hook Right before inserting, smear some milk around the outside of the nipple.

4. Commence Docking Maneuvers Sit with baby lying in the crook of your arm. Elevate her head. If you lay her flat, she is more susceptible to choking and ear infections. Activate the rooting reflex (see pages 10 and 68) and insert the bottle.

5. Feed To prevent gas pains, tilt the bottle at such an angle that milk completely fills the nipple. In the beginning, you may have to periodically remove it to let the kid catch up. And never prop up the bottle and leave the room. Always administer feedings yourself.

6. Burp You can burp after every two ounces or whenever she starts fussing.

Preparing Formula

Even if you haven't noticed any strange mutations in the local fauna, you should sterilize the water that you use in formula by boiling it. You can also use filtered water.

The easiest way to prepare formula is a six-pack at a time. Get a clean pitcher and mix in the correct ratio of formula to water (put the water in first to avoid clumping). Stir vigorously. Fill six empty bottles with the desired amount, put the caps on, and stick the bottles in a six-pack container. These bottles will remain usable for twenty-four hours.

Cleaning Bottle Parts

The CDC (not the Canadian Dairy Council, the other one) recommends you sterilize bottle parts once a day. Three possible ways to do this:

- put them through the dishwasher, using dishwasher-safe bottles and baskets for the nipples and rings
- boil them for five minutes
- buy a bottle washer and sterilizer, which many new parents consider a godsend

Sleeping Like a Baby

NIGHT OF THE LIVING DAD
Showtimes at 9:15, 9:34, 11:20, 11:27, 12:53

When you hear the phrase "newborn sleep patterns," disregard the word "patterns." Unless you invoke chaos theory, you may not see a pattern at all, at least for the first month or so. Your baby may sleep for five minutes or five hours. And when she graces you with a five-hour slumber, try to resist the urge to break out the confetti cannons, because chances are her next nap will last for exactly five minutes.

The deevolution of the exhausted dad

For the first three months, babies normally sleep about fourteen to seventeen hours a day. Sadly for you, they are not in a row. Typically she'll sleep in short spurts of two to four hours. This results in a very surreal time for new dads, because your day is broken up into something like eight identical mini-days, coming at irregular intervals, consisting solely of feeding, burping, changing, and putting her back to sleep. Days and nights bleed into one another. You're not sure when you last showered or ate or brushed your teeth. After a week or so, you develop the same look that you see on first-year medical residents.

Sleep Inducement Methods

The following are tips for getting your newborn to nod off. In a few months, you can wean her off these rituals and help her to sleep more independently. (Advanced sleep methods are covered on pages 142–46.)

Singing

Choose droning, monotonous songs like "100 Bottles of Beer," and gradually get softer and slower as you see the baby starting to tilt. To keep yourself from falling asleep in the process, choose a song like "The Wheels on the Bus," and add your own ridiculous lyrics. "The Chewbacca on the bus goes Rrrruuuurrr, Rrrruuuurrr, Rrrruuuurrr," "The Keanu on the bus drives fifty-plus."

Feeding

All that sucking tires babies out. Many times you'll notice, mid-snack, a drunken look on her face, and within seconds she'll be out.

Confinement

Accustomed to the womb, many babies equate comfort with confinement, and they'll sleep better if you find ways to pin them down, either with a swaddle (see page 60), or by putting them to sleep in the car seat.

Motion

Even before birth, your newborn fell into bad sleep habits. She was rocked to sleep in the womb by your partner's every movement, and now that she's on dry land, she will probably expect the same treatment. To keep her in perpetual motion, you can either go battery-powered, using the electronic swing or vibrating bouncy seat; gas- or electric-powered, taking the car out for long, slow trips around the block with her in the car seat; or dad-powered, rocking her in your arms (see next page for details) or walking around with her in the stroller or front carrier. Remember to always supervise a baby sleeping anywhere other than a flat crib.

Babies should not sleep in the car seat, stroller, swing, or bouncy seat for extended periods, so transfer her to the crib once she is in dreamland.

White Noise

White noise is an amazing sleep inducer. Not only does it mask unwanted outside sounds, rendering the baby oblivious to pinging phones, creaking doors, and barking dogs, but it also mimics the sound of the rushing fluids and shifting body weight that she heard in the womb. In one study, young babies were three times as likely to fall asleep while listening to white noise as those not exposed. You can buy a white noise machine or download one of the many apps.

And in a pinch, a household fan, air conditioner, or air purifier can do the job as well.

The Finger Forehead Maneuver

This trick seems like dark magic, but it works. Gently run your finger from the top of your baby's forehead to the tip of her nose. Repeat. For some reason, many munchkins find this very soothing, causing them to close their eyes, relax, and drift off. This technique has also been known to work on dogs and drunk people. But your results may vary.

For Those About to Rock

Pace Studies have shown that the most effective rocking mimics the mother's walking pattern, which is approximately sixty rocks per minute (rocking to the left and then to the right equals two rocks). This is a brisk pace compared to the slow, gentle tempo you might picture in your head, but let your baby be the judge. She'll let you know if you need to put on the brakes.

Music Babies are often comforted by strong, methodical beats. Some parents use metronomes to put their moppets to sleep, but in lieu of that, try music. Many Bob Marley songs have slow, steady rhythms that fit into the "sixty rocks per minute" range, including "Buffalo Soldier," "Jammin'," "Is This Love," "Exodus," and "No Woman, No Cry."

Since not all babies love reggae, here are some other songs that could also do the trick:

No Baby, No Cry

"Purple Rain"
Prince

"Kiss from a Rose"
Seal

"Landslide"
Fleetwood Mac

"Low Rider"
War

"Old Town Road"
Lil Nas X

"The Lion Sleeps Tonight"
The Tokens

"Seven Nation Army"
The White Stripes

"Comfortably Numb"
Pink Floyd

"Bad Medicine"
Bon Jovi

"Beyond the Sea"
Bobby Darin

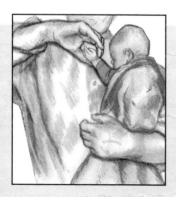

The Sleep Test
Before you lay the baby down, you've got to make sure that she's entered into a good, sound slumber. To test her level of sleepiness, lift one of her arms a couple of inches and then let it fall. (Think of a wrestling referee testing whether The Undertaker has squeezed the life out of Stone Cold Steve Austin.) If she offers any resistance, you've got some more work to do.

The Delicate Art of the Transfer

Transferring a sleeping baby to a crib is like defusing a bomb. It's a painstakingly delicate process. One false move and you've bought yourself another half hour of rocking. To ensure a smooth transition, follow the steps below:

1. While rocking, gently reposition your hands so that you'll be able to pull them out from under her, spatula-like, when you finally put her down.

2. Walk her slowly toward the crib or bed, rocking continuously. Search the floor for objects that could serve as tripping hazards or audible land mines, like a squeaky stuffie.

3. Once you are in front of the mattress, gradually let the rocking come to a halt.

4. Slowly lay her down on her back, keeping body contact for as long as you can (without compromising your back). Keep your hands under her body for a little while. This will help warm up the mattress.

5. As you pull away from her, transfer your hands onto her chest. Hold them there for another minute.

6. Take a deep breath and gently remove your hands. Then pray silently as you leave the room.

Dream Feeds

Once your baby is two to three months old, you can start administering "dream feeds," which could very well buy you and your partner a few bonus hours of uninterrupted shut-eye. For instance, say your baby goes down at 7:30 p.m., and you go to bed at 10:30 p.m. At 10 p.m., wake her just enough for another feeding to top her off. Even just a few sips could curb her appetite and grant you all some added Zs.

Baby Monitors

While it's true that parents survived without baby monitors for thousands of years, those parents didn't have a sixty-inch flat screen with a sound bar and wireless subwoofer. If your baby wakes up and starts crying, you'll want to be made aware. Before the due date, test out monitors with your partner. Have her stand in the baby's proposed sleep space and whine while you walk around the house and listen.

Baby monitors have gone super–high tech, with a wide range of features including two-way talk, temperature sensors, infrared night vision, breath-tracking, a white noise generator, multiple cameras, and 1080p screen resolution. Some send you a speed-motion summary of the baby's entire night, while others let you log in and monitor the baby remotely, which is a lot of fun for far-flung grandparents desperate for a baby fix.

Be warned that the night vision feature makes your baby's eyes glow. Pair that with the snorting, whistling, and grunting many infants produce during sleep, and it may seem like she needs an exorcist.

Hooking Up a Sidecar

With the co-sleeper, you can get some shut-eye and your partner can feed in bed.

If you'd like to keep the baby in the room with you (as is universally recommended), the co-sleeper, a.k.a. bedside crib, is a great option. Simply put, it's a three-walled crib that hooks on to the side of your bed. You can easily pull the baby into the big bed for feedings and escort her back into the co-sleeper when she's had her fill. And when she becomes more mobile, you can raise the fourth wall to keep her from trespassing into your bed.

The co-sleeper has an adjustable panel that raises and lowers.

Big Bed Baby?

The American Academy of Pediatrics warns against sharing your bed with the baby, citing the increased risk of accidental suffocation and SIDS-related death. That being said, recent surveys have shown that a majority of new parents do share the bed with the baby at some point, often simply due to convenience, exhaustion, and ease of breastfeeding. And some parents make a conscious choice to bed-share, citing studies suggesting it helps babies fall asleep more easily, encourages prolonged breastfeeding, and brings parents and babies closer together. But if you or your partner is obese, a smoker, an extremely deep sleeper, have sleep apnea, take sedatives, or drink to excess, you should definitely not have the baby in your bed.

Obviously this is a very serious consideration, and we encourage you to make your own informed decision. And if you do choose to bed-share, make sure to research ways to make it as safe as possible, including having a firm mattress and keeping all blankets and pillows out of baby's reach.

About SIDS Risks

New parents spend a great deal of time worrying about SIDS (Sudden Infant Death Syndrome). In truth, the risk is very, very low—less than 1 in 2,500, or .04%. And if you take these simple precautions, your risk will be much lower than that.

- Put the baby to sleep on her back.
- Use a firm mattress and a thin fitted sheet.
- Avoid overheating your baby.
- Share a room with your baby for the first six months.
- Don't use crib bumpers.
- Keep stuffed animals, pillows, comforters, and blankets out of her sleep space.
- Don't smoke, and keep the baby away from people who do.
- If possible, your partner should breastfeed.
- Take an infant CPR class.

Since research into SIDS is ongoing, consult your pediatrician for the latest facts.

Office Spaced

At some point you may find yourself punching out of baby world and back into work world for around eight hours a day. If you've taken advantage of the Family and Medical Leave Act, you can take up to twelve weeks of unpaid leave or arrange to work a temporary part-time schedule. Either way, your employer can't penalize you for taking time off to be with the baby. Some companies, however, are exempt from the FMLA, so make sure you're covered before barging into your boss's office and demanding your rights.

Sleep Deprivation

Exhaustion is by far the biggest obstacle you'll face as you reinsert yourself into the working world. You'll be doing the same tasks you used to, but they'll take twice as long. You'll read the same page three different times before comprehension kicks in. The basic rules of division and multiplication suddenly elude you. And forget about giving a presentation. The right words are always just out of reach.

Studies have shown that your IQ actually drops with each hour of sleep lost. Your language center starts to shut down, your memory becomes sluggish, reaction time slows, and you become irritable. The good news is that lack of sleep won't kill you (as long as you don't fall asleep while trucking, roofing, or lion taming).

There are ways to fight the effects of sleep deprivation. It's been proven that naps, even short catnaps, can do wonders for your mental agility. Researchers from NASA found that airline pilots who napped for an average of twenty-six minutes increased their alertness by 54% and job performance by 34%. (Presumably they weren't napping on the job.)

At home, siestas are acceptable. But unless you've got your own private office, you're going to have to find more innovative ways to catch some shut-eye.

Here are three possibilities:

- On your lunch break, go to your car, adjust your seat as far back as it can go, and drift off. (And if you don't have a car, there's usually an empty office or two.)

- If your workplace has a gym, you can lie down on a yoga mat and spend half an hour in the corpse pose.

- If you're really desperate, go into a stall in the men's room, take a seat, prop a roll of toilet paper under your neck like an airplane pillow, and shut your eyes.

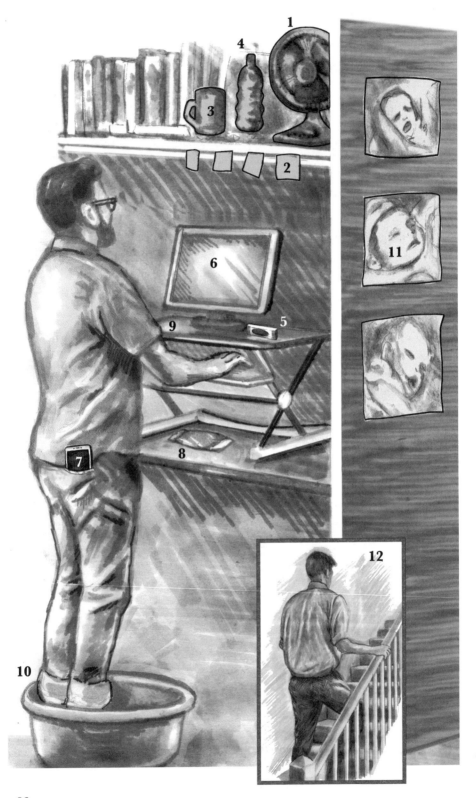

Tactics for Staying Upright at Your Desk

There are times when a nap is not an option, and you've just got to slog through the day somehow. Try these tactics for keeping conscious in your cubicle. Four or five of them, used in conjunction, just might do the trick.

1. An oscillating fan for a cool, irregular breeze

2. Sticky notes for everything (because you can't trust your brain)

3. Caffeine!

4. Water to help get your blood flowing and aid the circulatory system

5. Chewing gum (preferably peppermint or cinnamon, as they are natural stimulants)

6. Sharp, dissonant music (bagpipes are perfect)

7. Programmed phone alerts that vibrate in your pocket at regular intervals

8. A light lunch like fruit, nuts, yogurt, or energy bars (a heavy meal will tire you)

9. An adjustable standing desk to increase circulation

10. A tub of cold water for your bare feet (a bit preposterous, but it works like a charm)

11. A prominent display of baby photos to remind people to cut you some slack in case you actually do keel over onto your keyboard

12. Hourly breaks to climb stairs (which will oxygenate your blood)

13. Sticking your head out a window (sunlight boosts serotonin levels, which gives you energy)

13

Home Not Alone

Stay-At-Home Dads have been given the unfortunate acronym SAHDs. But working from home doesn't have to be sahd, as long as you've got the right plan, the right attitude, and the right noise-canceling headphones.

Dedicated Workspace

If possible, set up a dedicated workspace, preferably away from baby-heavy areas. With all the household entropy that comes with new parenting, it's much easier to know where all your work materials are located when you need them. When choosing a location, keep in mind where your web camera will be facing. You don't want your coworkers catching a glimpse of your partner sopping up a blowout while staring daggers into the back of your head.

And never, ever underestimate the value of a door. It might even be worth moving your office into a closet just to create a barrier from kid-related chaos during your dedicated working hours.

Diapers and Deadlines

Whether or not your partner is also working, at some point you will face the daunting task of working and caring for the baby at the same time. Accomplishing this feat requires planning, patience, and lowered expectations by all involved.

To set yourself up for success:

Become a Mute Master On a video meeting or conference call, stay on mute until the second you need to talk, and as soon as you're finished, mash that mute button so that your colleagues don't get an earful of a screaming baby or your exasperated partner loudly asking if you've seen the nipple cream.

Strap Her In Pop your little nugget into a baby carrier strapped to your chest as you tackle work tasks. This proves invaluable, particularly during those endless video meetings. Not only will your coworkers be treated to a dose of adorableness, but your boss will also be reminded that you're a multitasking superhero in need of a day off.

Carpe Napem Seize the snooze session by doing the bulk of your work while the baby naps. Pregame with a heavy dose of caffeine so you can launch like a rocket.

Go Hands-Free As your mitts may be full of baby, download dictation software so you can rock and work at the same time.

Back It Up Most computer manufacturers don't recommend baby vomit on a hard drive. Back everything up regularly.

Phone It In You can mirror your desktop onto your phone so that you'll be able to work lying down with a sleeping infant on your chest.

Reading EVERYTHING to Your Baby

Experts agree that reading to even very young sprogs is highly beneficial. Hearing words read aloud helps to map a baby's brain to focus on, and eventually recognize, certain sound patterns, the building blocks of language. It's basically *Reading Rainbow* for the newborn set.

Why not institute a daily dad-baby reading ritual as soon as possible? It'll be fun for the both of you, and although she can't tell a duck from a doorknob, hearing your voice will strengthen her connection to you and give her comfort.

As for reading material, baby books are great, but they can get tedious, and there are times when you'll want to switch things up. Since anything with words and bright images can do the trick, why not choose something that suits your interests?

Graphic Novels If you're a comic geek, why not expose the baby to some of your favorite titles? The joy and enthusiasm you show might spread to the little nipper.

Gossip Rags Next time you're in the checkout line, grab a copy of *People* or *Us Weekly*. You can catch up on celebrity breakups, and the baby can help you decide "Who Wore It Best?"

Sports Mags Baby will be attracted to the bright, contrasty uniforms (especially the refs), and en-thralled with your play-by-play commentary.

Baby Catalogs As soon as you become a parent, baby catalogs somehow just magically appear. And it will be nice to get a first glimpse of the equipment that you'll be tripping over in the coming months.

Cereal Boxes Cereal boxes are big, colorful, and usually have a ton of text on them. And at some point your kid's got to learn what riboflavin is.

Junk Mail Instead of chucking it straight into the recycling bin, why not read it to the pipsqueak? Peruse the real estate flyers and point out all the different fruits and vegetables in the supermarket circulars. You might actually find a few bargains. And the best part is, if the baby spits up on it, you were going to throw it out anyway.

A Guy's Guide to Strollers

Dads who don't go stroller shopping are missing out on a golden opportunity to throw around phrases like "turning radius," "spring-action suspension," and "off-road performance." And if you allow a relative to "gift" you a stroller, then you can't gripe when you find yourself trudging through the mall pushing an antique pram with a teddy-bear-printed canopy.

Three things you should do before buying any stroller:

Test Drive

Even if you are used to buying almost everything online, it's important to trudge out to a store and test out a few models. Assess maneuverability and performance in tight corners. Can you steer it effectively with one hand while holding a coffee? Are the handles high enough so that you aren't hunched over? Turn an aisle of the store into a slalom course where you can test the stroller's limits. And if you're at a big-box store, head over to the produce section and strap a watermelon into the seat to see how safely it stays in place at cruising speed.

Kick the Tires

Test the locking mechanism, reclining mechanism, and wheel brakes. Are they well made? User friendly? Is there a five-point safety harness? Shake the stroller to determine sturdiness. And most importantly, collapse and expand the unit. When stroller manufacturers boast the ability to fold and unfold with one hand, they often mean "besides the two you already have."

Lift and Carry

Would you be able to carry it up a flight of stairs? Would your partner be able to fold it up and hoist it into the trunk in a busy parking lot in the rain, or will she just leave it in the shopping cart corral? Remember that you guys will also be hauling diapers, wipes, toys, bottles, and up to twenty-five pounds of baby.

A few misguided parents think it's a good idea to "let the baby decide" by putting her in various models to see how she reacts. This is a very bad idea, mostly because babies cry for many different reasons, and what you think is a stroller rejection may just be gas.

A baby registry can be your best friend. Put in for your favorite stroller and all the accessories you need. Otherwise, you may end up with 500 pairs of newborn socks and no stroller.

The Six Basic Stroller Types

Make sure to get a stroller that folds down to fit in your trunk. (Never try this, of course.)

Convertible Strollers are baby carriages that can morph into strollers when the kid outgrows the built-in bassinet. Since babies under three months should be fully reclining (for head support), the bassinet strollers provide an ideal setting for the newborn. And the carriage configuration enables the parent and baby to face each other.

Some parents don't even bother with a stroller for the first few months, and use the carrier as their primary mode of baby transport.

Full-Size Strollers are large and roomy, and usually have a lot of bells and whistles, like full seat recline, seats that can be forward- or rear-facing, and roomy storage spaces. They tend to be on the heavy side (some are around twenty-five pounds), and can be a bit cumbersome to fold and expand.

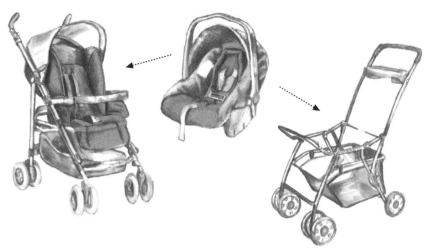

Travel Systems and Car-Seat Carriers provide several ways
to take your baby from the car into the stroller without removing
her from the seat. **Travel systems** are strollers with car seats
built into them. You can snap the car seat in and out pretty
quickly. One-piece systems have a collapsible frame and wheels
built into the car seat itself, turning your baby into an adorable
transformer. And **car-seat carriers** are simply frames with
wheels, and you just snap your own car seat into the frame.
(Gently lifting the car seat out of the car and into the stroller base
without waking up the baby is a feat few fathers have mastered.)

Lightweight Strollers (a.k.a. travel strollers)
weigh anywhere from fifteen to twenty pounds and
are great for urban dwellers. The best models are
surprisingly sturdy (and surprisingly expensive), and
offer easy open-and-fold technology. Many models
come with seats that fold all the way back so that
newborns can use them. The little wheels are a
drawback on rough terrain, and the
smaller storage basket forces some
parents to hang bags from the
handles, which can unbal-
ance the unit. (Attaching
your old wrist or ankle
weights to the front of
the frame can solve this
problem.)

*Lightweight strollers
can tip.*

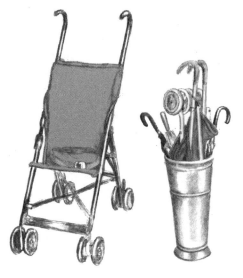

Umbrella Strollers could have gotten their name from their fold-ability, or the fact that they are about as sturdy as a street vendor umbrella. They are cheap, ultra-light, and ultimately disposable. Features include a piece of fabric over a frame. If you are traveling and need something really light to use in airports, these could do the trick. Otherwise, steer clear. While closing, they tend to collapse on your fingers.

Joggers are the Range Rovers of the stroller world. These three-wheeled beasts have a very high wheel base, which is opti-mal in the event of a stroller-on-stroller col-lision. They are perfect for extreme and wilderness strolling, but their size makes them less practical for everyday use. They shouldn't be used until babies can sup-port their heads. And no matter how gung ho you are about running, never buy a jogger until well after the baby is born. Then see how moti-vated you are. More often than not, joggers become hampers as soon as baby arrives.

Some Useful Accessories

• Plastic Rain Hood

• Boot (protects baby's feet in cold weather)

• UV Canopy (for sun protection)

• Cup Holder

• Activity Tray with Snack Holder

Tot Couture

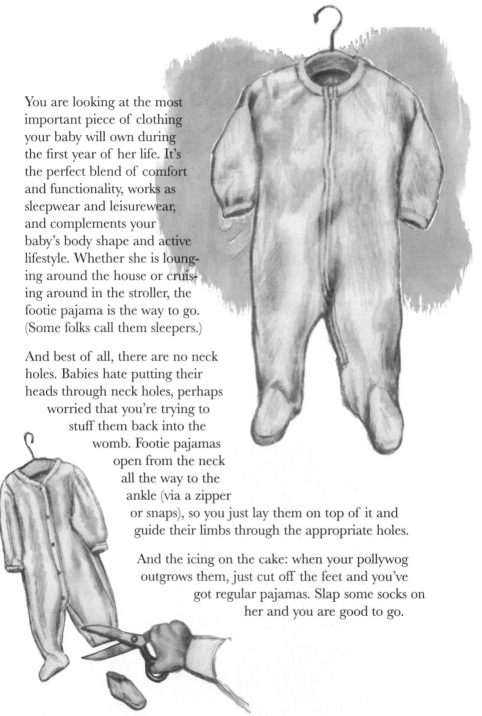

You are looking at the most important piece of clothing your baby will own during the first year of her life. It's the perfect blend of comfort and functionality, works as sleepwear and leisurewear, and complements your baby's body shape and active lifestyle. Whether she is lounging around the house or cruising around in the stroller, the footie pajama is the way to go. (Some folks call them sleepers.)

And best of all, there are no neck holes. Babies hate putting their heads through neck holes, perhaps worried that you're trying to stuff them back into the womb. Footie pajamas open from the neck all the way to the ankle (via a zipper or snaps), so you just lay them on top of it and guide their limbs through the appropriate holes.

And the icing on the cake: when your pollywog outgrows them, just cut off the feet and you've got regular pajamas. Slap some socks on her and you are good to go.

Now, your partner may try to throw the concept of aesthetics into the mix, choosing, against all logic, to bedeck the baby in jumpers and rompers and tights and leggings, things from Italy with tiny neck holes and inaccessible crotches. These outfits admittedly make your baby look fetching, but (a) tots hate getting into them and (b) you might want to avoid any baby clothes that require dry cleaning. Your little princess is expensive enough.

Babies don't enjoy being dressed like a sailor in a Broadway musical

Dressing for Hot and Cold

Your baby doesn't need any more clothing than you do, and she'll usually tell you, by fussing, if she's uncomfortable. If you want a gauge, check the back of her neck. If it feels either too cold or hot and sweaty, adjust clothing accordingly. Other signs of overheating include damp hair, hot ears, and clammy skin.

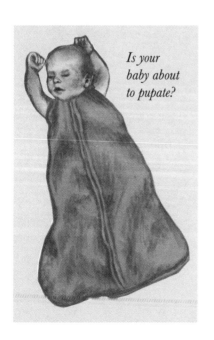

Is your baby about to pupate?

In cold weather, it's best to dress her in layers that you can take off and put on as the temperature shifts. And if she needs mittens, stick a pair of baby socks on her hands.

Winter Sleeping

When the temperature drops, you may need a layer over your baby's footie pajamas at bedtime, but blankets have been deemed unsafe for young ones. That's where the sleep sack (a.k.a. wearable blanket) comes in. A sleeveless, collarless potato sack of a garment, the wearable blanket keeps her warm, toasty, and safe, while making her look like a giant larva.

The Sun

Treat your baby like a vampire for the first six months, keeping her out of direct sunlight as much as possible. When you do go out with her, try to cover her up with loose, long-sleeve clothing.

Once she hits six months, you can venture out into the sun for limited periods, but be sure to slather baby sunscreen on all unclothed areas. Also get a pair of sunglasses to protect her eyes, but don't be surprised if they wind up on the ground more than on her face. A lightweight flap hat (see above) will also keep out the glare and protect her head and neck in the process.

Summer Sleeping

What do you do when it's too hot for footie pajamas? Try this little number here. It's called a onesie, and it's a no-brainer. Loose neck, crotch snaps—what's not to like? Unsnapped, it looks like your baby's wearing tails.

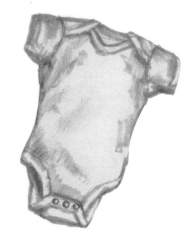

And if the neck hole is too small, you can stretch it around a half-gallon plastic soda bottle for a couple of hours to loosen it up.

4–6 MONTHS

Sanity Maintenance

You've probably begun to realize that most of the time spent with babies is not so much quality time as it is *quantity* time—endless hours of routine bodily maintenance, punctuated by knee-bouncing, song-singing, and the occasional staring contest. You check the time thinking that hours have gone by, and mere minutes have ticked off.

The isolation and lack of mental stimulation can start to make you loopy. You may find yourself eagerly answering spam calls, excited for any grown-up conversation. You'll stare at a baby video for ten minutes after your little one's asleep on your lap. Before long, you are ending all of your adult interactions with a high-pitched "bye-bye." Is your brain starting to curdle? And what can you do about it?

"I'd LOVE to talk about my vehicle's lapsed warranty."

Stay Informed

Life with a baby is life in a vacuum. There is a whole world out there, and although you may find it hard to believe, your baby's poop schedule is not international news. Keep yourself connected by reading the news whenever you get a chance. (And by news, we mean reliable sources.) This way, the next time you converse with an adult, you'll have something to contribute besides the latest breast pump technology. Also, feel free to read articles to your baby in a singsongy tone. Of course, he won't know what the heck you're talking about, but just the sound of your voice will be soothing.

Maintain Your Fighting Weight

Some dads experience their sympathetic pregnancy after the baby comes, a result of eating odd things at odd hours and getting almost no exercise. But it's important to stay within range of your pre-baby weight, for several reasons. Being overweight can lead to back pain, which is exacerbated by constant bending to pick up the scamp and his gear. And once he starts to crawl, you'll inevitably have to leap up, Spider-Man-like, to grab the remote before it hits the toilet bowl.

Get Out!

When you're stuck indoors, time can feel slower than a snail in a snow-storm. Pack him up and go somewhere. Anywhere. Take a trip to the auto parts store. Let him feel some tire tread and look at all the shiny hubcaps, at the same time giving your partner some much-needed peace and solitude.

Don't Abandon Your Hobbies

Try to remember what you enjoyed doing in your free time before the baby arrived. Did you play video games, build Legos, whittle, juggle, bake, or decoupage? Carve out a little downtime during the week for a hobby. It will help you decompress.

Keep Your Close Friends Close

In a study of over 4,000 new dads, 20% reported losing close friends during the first year. You might not be available for softball leagues or game nights, but really close friends will understand and adapt to your new situation. Seize the chance to reconnect. Take a hike, go for a coffee with your little one strapped in, or invite them along for a diaper dash to the bodega.

Find Other New Dads

If you want to feel better about your brand-new life, don't exclusively hang out with child-free folks. Even though you keep telling yourself their lives are empty and devoid of higher purpose, it's hard not to get jealous of their insane amount of freedom and energy that they totally take for granted. Instead, spend some time with other new dads. Exhaustion loves company. Where can you find them? Just look in their natural habitats—the baby aisle at the supermarket, the pediatrician's office, the playground, or slumping next to a stroller at Starbucks. But probably the easiest way to connect with them is online. Search for new dad groups in your area on the social app of your choosing. Many groups have weekly or monthly meetups.

And once you find your pack, get a dad group chat going, so you can vent among friends.

BRAG RACE
In every new dad group, there's always that one blowhard who can't help but go on and on about his baby's incredible accomplishments. Miraculously, the baby never cries, sleeps like a champ, spouts words like "cabernet" and "Montessori," and has already been scouted by pro baseball teams and child modeling agencies. Is it genetics? Luck? Or just a giant load of horse poop? Probably the latter. Regardless, don't let his tales get under your skin. Every baby develops at their own pace.

Resuming a Sex Life

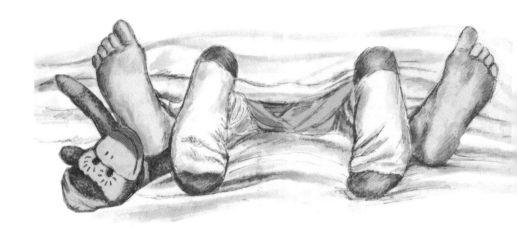

Though you are spending most of your energy trying to solve the Rubik's cube that is your baby, at some point during the first few months, your mind may wander back to the thing that got you here in the first place: sex.

How long should you wait after delivery to resume sex? While there is no definitive timeline, experts recommend waiting until your partner gets the green light at her six-week postnatal checkup.

And even if you do get the all clear, that doesn't necessarily mean you'll be ripping each other's clothes off in the car on the way home. Remember—like crawling, walking, and babbling, sex happens on its own time. A recent survey of almost 500 new moms found that about a quarter had sex before the six-week mark, with another quarter resuming at exactly six weeks. And the largest group (about 40%) waited between six weeks and seven months. Patience is key.

The worst thing you can do is put undue pressure on her, so don't be a horny jerk. Be the caring and chivalrous lug that she decided to make a baby with nine months ago. And remember these three things: (1) you've had long droughts before this and you've survived, (2) clear your search history, and (3) seriously, always clear your search history.

Why Your Partner May Be Giving You the Cold Shoulder

- Her hormones are suppressing her sex drive, making sure she cares for this baby instead of creating a new one.

- Her body's just pulled off a Houdini-like feat, and is healing.

- She may also be self-conscious about her body due to changes brought on by pregnancy. Do everything in your power to remind her that you find her attractive.

- She's been kneaded, pawed, and sucked on all day, and she may not want to be kneaded, pawed, and sucked on by anyone else for a while.

Regreasing the Wheels

The prepared dad knows that foreplay doesn't begin in the bedroom, and it doesn't begin right before sex.

- Set aside one night a week where you and your partner can be baby-free, even for just an hour or two. Take a walk, grab a taco, or get a sitter and just hang out in the next room with the door closed.

- Humor is a great aphrodisiac. Perform an elaborate mating ritual dance reminiscent of the sage grouse. Or surprise her by writing little love notes on the baby's diaper with a Sharpie. (But make sure your partner will be the next one to change him, and not your mother-in-law.)

- Remember that intimacy can be as important as sex. You may be going against millions of years of male heredity, but pressuring your partner in any way will do you no good and may reset the shot clock. At this point, let a cuddle be an end rather than a means.

- Drop subtle hints. You can say things like, "I read some-where that sex has been shown to reduce stress and ease back and neck pain. Not only that, but it also can help your skin retain elasticity and retard the aging process. Isn't that interesting?" By the way, all of this is true.

- Aphrodisiacs come in many different forms. Your partner catching a glimpse of you wash-ing breast pump pieces at the sink might have the same effect as her watching Ryan Gosling doing naked Pilates.

The Big Night (Or Morning, Afternoon...Whenever)

When will she be ready to unfreeze your membership card? It's hard to tell. Never assume that today's the day, but always be prepared just in case.

- Keep up with grooming rituals. Shave, shower, and manscape whenever possible. Ensure those chompers are brushed and keep your clothes reasonably fresh-smelling and spit-up-free.

- Swing through the R-rated aisle of your local drugstore. Stock up on lubricants (absolutely essential for postpartum sex), condoms (she can get pregnant again sooner than you think), and mood enhancers such as candles and massage oils. Grab a bottle of wine on the way out, and don't make eye contact with the clerk.

- Never, ever wake your partner for sex. It's like taking food away from a grizzly.

- Sweep the area for baby toys. You don't want to roll over mid-session and activate Elmo's "I love you" song.

- Time your sexcapade to coincide with your baby's deepest sleep state, which on average starts around twenty minutes after you put him down. But beware that babies have a sixth sense when it comes to their parents' sexual activity, choosing the most inopportune moments to wake up and start wailing. Perhaps their instincts are telling them to eliminate potential competition.

- Be prepared to call an audible. If traditional intercourse isn't feeling right, remember that there are plenty of other options.

And once you resume a sex life, don't be afraid to schedule it. The baby brings more than enough spontaneity into your lives. Waiting for a natural impulsive moment when you both feel rested and sexy may be a quixotic quest. Establishing a set time can ease any awkwardness, give you time to prepare, and even build excitement and anticipation. While it might feel oddly corporate, rest assured you won't be called in to HR.

/	Thursday	F
5	Throwdown Thursday	6
12		13

Shoring Up Your Core

Expect the bulk of the heavy lifting, lugging, and dragging to rest squarely on your sturdy shoulders. You'll tote the baby for long stretches, haul around his multitudinous gear, bend and twist to get him in and out of the car seat, wrestle the stroller out of the trunk, and occasionally scoop up your partner just to reassure her that she's still the Barbie to your Ken.

Is it any wonder that almost 40% of men experience back pain during their prime child-raising years?

Joining a gym at this point would most likely be an act of blind optimism, and may be frowned upon by your overwhelmed, under-exercised partner. This means that you've got to find a way to shore up your back while on the baby clock. And since he's basically a cuddly kettlebell, it's easy to integrate him into your workout. Here are some exercises to get you started.

Sticker Twist Crunches

Muscles Used: Abs, Obliques

1. Affix a big happy face sticker to each of your elbows.

2. Lie on your back with your knees bent and your feet on the floor.

3. Place the baby against your thighs and hold him steady with your right hand, while placing your left hand slightly behind your head, fingers touching your ears.

4. Slowly bring your left elbow toward the baby until your shoulder comes off the floor. Try to bring the sticker about twelve inches away from his face.

5. Hold for three seconds while squeezing your abs, and then lower your back down to the floor.

6. Repeat, and then switch elbows.

Start out with two sets of ten reps each.

Car Seat Bends *Muscles Used: Obliques*

1. Stand with your feet about shoulder width apart and your back straight.

2. Hold the car seat (with the baby strapped in) in your left hand. Place your right hand on your waist.

3. Slowly bend to the side, and then return to starting position.

Start out with two sets of ten reps on each arm.

Carrier Wall Slides
Muscles Used: Back, Hips, Quadriceps

1. With your baby in the carrier, stand with your back against a wall and your feet shoulder width apart.

2. Slide down the wall until your knees are bent at a 45- to 60-degree angle. Keep your abdominals tight.

3. Count to five and slide back up.

Start with two sets of five to ten reps each, and slowly increase the number and duration of reps. This exercise gets much more difficult as the baby grows.

Plank 'n' Play *Muscles Used: Abs and Core Muscles*

1. With the baby on a mat directly beneath you, put a toy between your teeth and get into a push-up position, with hands directly below your shoulders.

2. Engage your ab muscles, drawing your navel toward your spine.

3. Do your best to keep your torso rigid and your body in a straight line from your ears to your toes.

4. Keep your shoulders down, not creeping up toward your ears.

You become a human mobile.

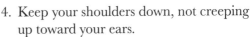

Hold this pose for fifteen seconds. Start with three sets, and then slowly increase the duration as you strengthen your core.

Circuit Training
Your Baby

LIFT.
NAP.
REPEAT.

Hanging out with the rug rat and looking for a good way to kill half an hour? Try setting up all of his gear in the living room and have him do a little circuit training. As his personal trainer, you'll guide him through each station of this CrossFit-style workout, shouting motivational phrases like "All you, all day!" and "Embrace the grind!"

As you may be aware, circuit training is a series of exercises designed to give you a quick and effective full-body workout. The baby circuit works the same way. When your tot has completed the workout, he'll have developed his muscles, coordination, and balance. Keep up the routine, and you'll have the buffest baby in the sandbox.

Spend a few minutes at each station with a short break in between. And if your small fry starts to get restless before he's completed the circuit, preempt the workout and go straight to the cooldown. That six-month six-pack will have to wait until next time.

If you're missing some gear from the circuit, don't worry—it won't throw off the workout. Simply skip to the next exercise on the list. And if you see a piece you'd like to add to your collection, consider browsing for a "gently used" one online.

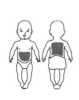

1st
STOP

The ExerSaucer is a two-tiered contraption with a round base and a cloth seat. Babies are positioned upright, which helps develop core muscles (abs and back).

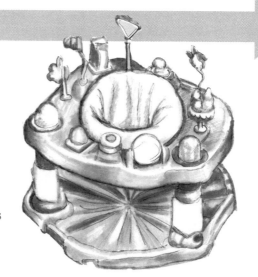

The Play Gym combines a play mat with a crossbar. There are holes at various points in the crossbar, allowing you to hang toys above your baby so he can reach up and touch/swat them. As he swings his arms, he's developing biceps, triceps, and gross motor skills.

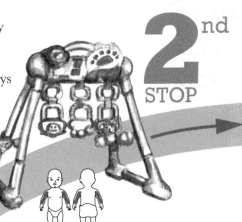

2nd
STOP

7th
STOP

The Swing or bouncer is the perfect relaxing cooldown.

The Boppy Pillow helps to support the baby as he learns to sit. Place him seated in this pillow with some favorite toys in front of him. Helps develop back and abdominal muscles.

6th
STOP

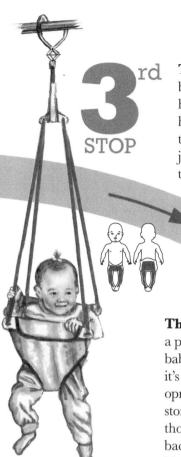

3rd STOP

The Jumper is a bucket seat tethered to a bungee cord that's hung in a doorway. You'll have fun watching your little one bounce his heart out. While it's tempting to leave him in there when he is having a blast, overuse of the jumper can be hard on the joints. This works the baby's glutes, quads, and calf muscles.

4th STOP

The Play Mat Face down on a play mat might not be every baby's cup of tea . . . however, it's important for their development. When he's on his stomach, he's forced to work those neck and back muscles to lift his head and look around.

5th STOP

The Kicking Piano (or Kick & Play) is a keyboard, often sold with a play mat, that sounds a note whenever the baby kicks a key. Good for lower-body strength and gross motor skills, and learning a few Billy Joel solos.

Tethering Everything to the Baby

Throwing things must be intensely satisfying for tots—watching the object disappear, hearing the thud/splat, catching Dad's animated reaction, and then seeing it reappear on the horizon.

Until you find a way to batten down everything in his immediate vicinity, you'll have to deal with his tendency to heave everything he can get his gooey little fingers around. This results in bottles and pacifiers covered in dirt, toys abandoned in mall parking lots, and bowls of mush splattered all over the kitchen floor. It's your first game of catch, and it's not nearly as fun as you imagined.

The good news is there are many different fastening options available (see below), and pretty much every object can be secured either to the baby or whatever contraption he happens to be inhabiting at the moment.

A word of caution: If you are thinking about making your own cords, keep in mind that anything over five inches long is considered a strangulation hazard.

   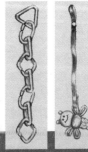

suction cup bowls   suction cup toys   pacifier cords   bottle holders   plastic baby links   toy straps

Germs & The Five-Second Rule

The Five-Second Rule has been accepted by many fathers as gospel. You know how it goes: If the baby drops something on the floor, and you pick it up within five seconds, the object is not yet officially "dirty." However, once you have passed the five-second mark, wash that sucker.

The exact truth, like the tops of a baby's ears, is a bit fuzzy.

The Clinical Study A Rutgers University study found that when microorganisms were spread on various flooring surfaces, they transferred to dropped objects almost instantaneously. That said, research has shown that floors have relatively low levels of bacteria, and your baby is far more likely to get sick the old-fashioned way: by putting his hands in his mouth, rubbing his eyes, or exposure to other sick people.

So, although the probability of your little one becoming ill from something dropped on the floor is relatively low, you should err on the side of caution and throw a package of baby wipes in your gear bag. His immune system is still developing, and on the off chance that he does drop a toy on a spot where there's harmful bacteria, that bacteria is definitely going to end up on the toy.

The Third Child It's common knowledge that parents get lazier and lazier with each child, and by the third, very little sterilization is going on. As one dad put it, "When our first dropped the pacifier, I'd run it under soap and water before giving it back to him. With our second, I'd wipe it off on my shirt. With the third, I just kick it back to him." Yet these third children seem to turn out just as healthy and robust as their more sanitized siblings. Consider that only the firstborn of the Manning Brothers failed to play in the NFL.

Daycare Is Undefeated It's important to acknowledge an unavoidable reality. Daycare centers, ball pits, and playgrounds are all basically giant petri dishes where babies swap microbes like tweens swap Pokémon cards. Your kiddo will generously share these microbes with you, instantly transforming your home into an infirmary.

And lastly, there's reason to believe that a more relaxed approach may not be such a bad thing. A 2014 Johns Hopkins study found that children exposed to dirt, dander, and germs were less likely to develop allergies and asthma later in life. Ultimately, the science is ever-evolving, so stay sane and pick your battles.

Temperature Taking Tactics

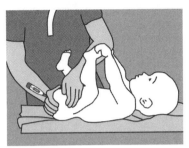

Figure 1

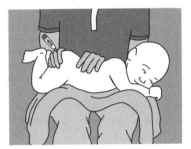

Figure 2

There are a number of ways to take a baby's temperature, with varying degrees of accuracy. Options include ear thermometers, forehead thermometers, pacifier thermometers, fever strips, smartphone apps, the hand-on-the-forehead technique, and digital thermometers that can be used rectally or under the armpit. At this age, taking your baby's temperature orally is not an option.

Doctors agree that the most accurate of the bunch is the digital rectal thermometer. They are fairly easy to use and have flexible rubber tips for safety. (Always sterilize thermometers between uses.)

- Place the baby either on a changing table on his back (figure 1), or across your lap on his belly (figure 2). Use the non-thermometer hand to help secure him.

- Lubricate the tip of the thermometer with petroleum jelly.

- Spread the cheeks and insert the thermometer tip ½ inch to an inch into the rectum. (Stop if you feel any resistance.)

- Hold it in place by laying your hand flush against your baby's buttocks with the thermometer between the index and middle fingers. This way if the baby bucks, your hand and the thermometer will move with him.

- When you hear the beep(s), remove the thermometer and apologize profusely to the baby.

If your wiggleworm is particularly annoyed by this procedure (and let's face it, who wouldn't be?), and insists on writhing around and kicking his legs, here is a dad-proven technique for holding him steady during the occupation.

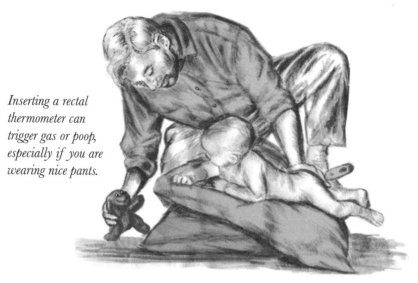

Inserting a rectal thermometer can trigger gas or poop, especially if you are wearing nice pants.

1. Place two pillows on top of one another on the floor, and lay a towel over the pillows.

2. Take off the baby's diaper and lay him face down with his stomach on top of the pillows. Spread his cheeks and insert the thermometer.

3. Use the other hand to animate a toy or stuffed animal, making it dance around, sing, and talk to the baby until you hear the beep.

Treating a Fever

A fever by itself isn't the best gauge of a baby's health. Behavior changes—listlessness, crankiness, nonstop crying—are even better indicators of a sick baby, and should be dealt with by calling the pediatrician.

Regarding a fever, here is a general guideline.

If he's UNDER two months old and has a temperature of 100.4°F or above, it's generally best to go to the emergency room, because it could be an indication of something more serious.

If he is OVER two months old and has a temp of 100.4°F or above, it's a bit more of a gray area. If the fever is accompanied by dehydration, trouble breathing, inability to be soothed, or if he is too sleepy to feed, go to the emergency room. Otherwise, call the pediatrician.

Getting the Medicine Down

It feels good to torment Baby Shark.

If you want to earn your stripes as a dad, you've got to become a first-class medicine giver. This will involve smarts, stamina, and, at times, outright treachery, because the baby will almost surely put up resistance.

As this can be a messy procedure, put some towels down under the area. And prop the baby up to limit the risk of choking.

Some Proven Techniques

Gamify It "See, medicine is fun! Yay medicine!" Take turns "feeding" the meds to your partner, yourself, a stuffed animal, and then baby.

Mask the Taste Some medicines can be mixed with food (check with the pharmacist). Stir it into a spoonful of applesauce or mix it with a small amount of milk in the baby's bottle. Or make it super cold (dulling its taste) and add a dash of sugar.

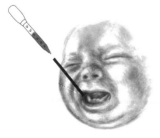

Bypass the Buds Using a dropper or syringe, aim for the area between the cheek and lower gum, toward the back (see image). If you are lucky, the medicine may just slide right down his throat without incident.

Bait and Switch Feed the baby ice cream, and after five or six bites, when his mouth's open wide, quickly shoot in a stream of medicine followed by a quick spoonful of ice cream. He may not know what hit him.

Resort to Deceit If you are desperate, you can try the Trojan horse method—a modified pacifier that, once inside baby's mouth, squirts medicine. But be warned: he may become incensed by this betrayal, as the pacifier was one of the few reliable things in his life. A similar method involves placing the syringe inside a bottle nipple and using his sucking instinct to take in the meds.

Change Flavors, Strengths, or Forms Meds come in a multitude of flavors, so if one doesn't work, try another. And some prescriptions come in different strengths. Always opt for the stronger dosage, because that means you'll have to give the baby less of it. Or you may choose to bypass the mouth entirely if suppositories are available.

Medicine and the Ornery Baby

Some babies just don't know what's good for them. Since there's no choice but to get the medicine down, you may have to channel your inner cowboy and resort to the steer rustler technique.

1. Prop a pillow up against one arm of the couch, and spread out a towel for stain control.

2. Wrap the youngster in a blanket, pinning his hands against his sides.

3. Place his back up against the pillow.

4. Leaning over him, gently but firmly hold his chin steady with one hand while squirting a small amount of medicine into his cheek pocket with the other.

5. Gently blow into the baby's face. This triggers the Diving Reflex, which forces him to swallow.

6. Repeat steps 4 and 5 until all of the medicine is gone.

7. Thank the baby and tell him to see the receptionist on the way out to take care of his co-pay.

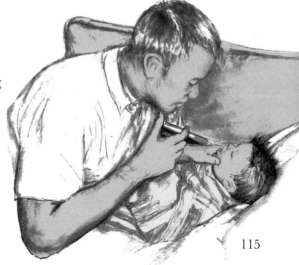

115

Droolapalooza

Michelangelo's
"The Teethers"

If your baby starts drooling uncontrollably, becomes irritated for no apparent reason, wakes up every hour, and tries to gum everything in sight, congratulations are in order! He's entering the ranks of the toothed.

But celebrating this new milestone is probably the last thing on your mind. "Why me?" is more like it. Just when you start breathing a little sigh of relief—the baby is sleeping for longer stretches, you and your partner are back on speaking terms—the onset of teething is an abrupt reminder that serenity is a fragile and fleeting concept.

On average, a baby's first chopper arrives at around six months old, and girls tend to sprout a tooth a bit before boys do. Symptoms of teething usually appear about a week before the tooth actually rears its pointy little head (you can sometimes feel a bump just under the gum). Along with the symptoms listed above, he may also display red cheeks, a chin rash, a low-grade fever, irritated gums, tugging on his ears, and a refusal to feed.

But by far the most obvious sign is the absurd volume of spittle streaming down his chin at all times, making him look like one of those tacky cherub fountains you find in some people's backyards. He may soak through five or six outfits a day.

Be aware that these symptoms can be indicative of other conditions as well, so if they persist, or if you have any concerns, call your pediatrician

Your Teething Toolbox

When your parents were teething, your grandparents might have rubbed whiskey on their gums, a proven old country remedy that doctors today do not prescribe. Perhaps they're afraid you'll give your baby crib spins, or they fear you'll self-medicate and pass out on his changing table. The truth is that alcohol is a toxin, and too much could harm the baby.

Since a highball is out of the question, here are some alternate offerings:

Your Knuckles and Fingers Your knuckles seem to be the perfect size and firmness for chewing, and applying gentle pressure on the afflicted area with your finger can also provide relief. Or try a little baby toothbrush that fits over your finger. The bristles soothe the teething itch.

Teething Toys Many teething toys have bumps and nodules for the wee one to chew on, but some young teethers may not have the dexterity to hold them in place.

Random Cold Objects When chilled, almost any object can become a teething toy. Spoons, bananas, bagels, full-size carrots, silicone spatulas, pacifiers, and clean, wet washcloths can be slightly frozen and given to the bambino to gnaw on. Note that items that are completely frozen solid are too hard and can bruise the gums. Always supervise him when he's teething on foods to make sure no pieces break off, especially once the first tooth pokes through.

Frozen bagels can be tethered to the baby, stroller, or high chair.

teething mitt

She's signaling for a spitball.

Mesh Feeders are pacifier-shaped devices with the rubber tip replaced by a mesh sack that you fill with frozen breast milk, ice cubes, fruit, etc. The feeder ensures that your baby won't swallow any large chunks. In a pinch, you can make your own feeder out of a super-clean gym sock filled with frozen ice, fruit, or breast milk, and then knotted.

Teething Mitts are basically thumbless catcher's mitts with rubber nubs on the fingertips for the baby to gnaw on. A Velcro strap secures it to the hand.

Acetaminophen is perhaps the most effective way to deal with nighttime teething issues. Baby acetaminophen—or as it's known on the streets, Liquid Nap—works for up to four hours, giving you at least a shot at three hours and fifty-nine minutes of sleep. Make sure to consult your pediatrician before giving the baby any medicine. (For help getting medicine into your baby, see pages 114–15.)

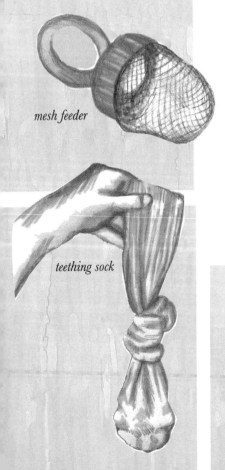

mesh feeder

teething sock

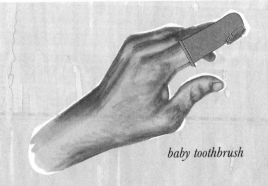

baby toothbrush

Tooth Maintenance

You wouldn't wash your car on the way to the junkyard. So why would you take care of a baby tooth if it's just going to fall out anyway? Well, here are three important reasons why tooth maintenance needs to be an important part of your routine:

- Baby teeth don't fall out for another five years, so if you want your baby to enjoy a nice juicy steak one day, you'd better take care of those chompers now.

- Brushing baby teeth prevents cavities and gum disease.

- Baby teeth are placeholders for adult teeth, and losing them early could cause future crowding and spacing issues.

- Unless he plans on going into hip-hop, it would be a bit startling for your baby's only tooth to have a big gold cap on it.

To keep his tooth clean, you can gently brush it daily with a baby toothbrush topped with a dab of baby toothpaste. Also, don't let him sleep for long periods with a bottle or breast in his mouth because the sugar from the milk can cause decay. And when he hits the one-year mark, take a trip to the pediatric dentist.

Order of Tooth Development

1s erupt between 6 and 10 months
2s erupt between 8 and 12 months
3s erupt between 9 and 13 months
4s erupt between 10 and 16 months

This is just an average. Some babies don't get a tooth until after their first birthday, and a few even come out of the womb flashing a pearly white. (The tooth is often removed so it won't fall out and become a choking hazard.)

Be Prepared
for
OUTINGS

Getting out of the house with a baby is like moving the pope. There is a ridiculous amount of paraphernalia that you have to lug around. And for some reason, the size of the baby is inversely proportional to the weight of the load.

One of the biggest advantages many dads have over moms is our ability to exit the house quickly. That is because dads embrace one of the cardinal laws of parenthood:

Once you've managed to get out of the house with the baby, DON'T go back in no matter what.

If you've forgotten something, either buy a new one or take your chances without it. But if you make it a policy to keep going back for stuff, eventually you'll become paralyzed with indecision and you'll never leave.

You might get a case of the cold sweats when faced with your first solo field trip with the small fry. After all, you haven't even mastered in-home care, where there's plenty of food, shelter, equipment, and immediate access to emergency services. So what makes you think you can survive in the field? In a word, preparation!

Your Gear Bag

There are hundreds of diaper bags on the market, including many advertised as "dad bags"—rugged-looking, military-inspired backpacks with pouches and compartments made from "tactical polyester." But you don't need to spend hundreds of dollars on a diaper bag when any old backpack will do.

Eight Essential Items to Put in Your Gear Bag

1. **Diapers** One for every hour you'll be out, and at least two more than you think you'll need.

2. **Wipes** for everything from fluid containment to stain removal to cleaning off your own grubby hands.

3. **Dog Poop Bags** conveniently come in compact rolls, and are specifically designed to contain poop and poop odors. They can hold everything from used diapers to wipes to soiled clothes. You can also use them as makeshift gloves when dealing with a particularly hazmatty situation. And many are biodegradable.

4. **Changing Pad** to put down under the baby during diaper swaps. (And no, a Taco Bell wrapper doesn't count.)

5. **Beverages** Breast milk can be stored in bottles along with cold packs in a small bottle bag. Powdered formula can be put in a ziplock bag and poured into bottles full of water, or you can purchase premade formula bottles. And don't forget water for you.

6. **Burp Cloths** so you won't walk around smelling like spit-up.

7. **Clothes** for you and baby. Pack at least two complete outfits for him and an extra shirt for you just in case.

8. **Toys** provide stimulation or distraction to head off a crying jag.

Instead of memorizing the full list, you can memorize this handy acronym. The first letter of each word is also the first letter of an item on the list.

"Dad's Back Discomfort Caused By Carrying Weighty Tot."

Before you venture out with your bag, do a dry run at home. Simulate changing a diaper in the field, holding the baby down with one hand while taking out all your supplies with the other. This will give you a good sense of where to place each item in the backpack for easiest access.

And always restock your gear bag when you get home, so you'll be ready to go at a moment's notice.

Supplementary Items

Because you ought to be prepared for everything, you may want to take along the following additional materials:

Multi-Tool Pocket tools like the Leatherman are useful for everything from opening formula to stroller repairs.

Duct Tape Good for stroller and carrier repair, emergency diaper fastening, etc.

Extra Pacifiers Even if you have one tethered to his shirt, it's always good to have an extra three or four.

Key Chain Toy It may look goofy, but clip a toy or small stuffed animal to the outside of the backpack. For situations where you need immediate distraction, it's the ace in your deck.

Hand Sanitizer You won't always have access to soap and water.

Snacks for You The baby is not the only one who has hunger tantrums.

Mini First-Aid Kit Includes a variety of Band-Aids, gauze, alcohol wipes, tweezers.

Baby Hat and Sunblock Important for outdoor treks.

Phone Charger You never know when you'll need to call for backup.

Up until now, you could take your baby just about anywhere and he'd probably have a similar stone-faced reaction. But by 4–6 months, his burgeoning personality is starting to reveal itself, and he will definitely prefer some activities over others.

Supermarkets The dazzling array of colors, textures, and sounds will really excite your newbie. Have him feel different products—a crinkling bag of chips versus a cold frozen turkey. Satisfy his urge to drop things by letting him toss items into the cart. And definitely try to catch the misting of the produce. It's the baby version of the Bellagio fountains.

Pet Stores The chirping birds, gurgling fish tanks, hamsters, and lizards can be captivating. It's like a free zoo! If you feel guilty about loitering, buy a squeaky dog toy for the imp to play with (but make sure it's baby-safe).

Escalators Riding up and down escalators helps with his growing sense of depth perception and object tracking, and he'll be sure to get smiles and waves from everyone coming the other way. (Never use the stroller on an escalator.)

Art Museums Most babies enjoy realism, especially portraits of people and animals. Sculpture also engages them, as do paintings with large clean shapes.

Happy Hour Bars cater to single people, for whom the baby is a novelty, so he'll likely get a lot of attention. But the place has got to be smoke-free, and you need to arrive before people are hammered and leave before the baby gets cranky.

Driving and CRYING

When you've got a baby in the car, you drive with a sense of purpose normally associated with ambulance drivers and carjackers. You know that at any moment things could go sideways. And if you have ever been trapped alone in a traffic jam with a screaming little demon in the back seat, then you know what desperation feels like.

If you're on your own, there are times when you need to stop the car to remedy the situation. If he's wet, you have to change him. If he's hungry, you have to give him a bottle. If he's bothered by the glare, you can attach a sun visor to the window. But for general fussiness, you can alleviate back-seat blubbering by employing the following tactics:

- Buy a baby car mirror that attaches to the back-seat headrest. The mirror enables you to see the baby and him to see your face in the rearview. There are dozens of options. Some even light up and play songs.

- Keep a large bin full of toys next to you in the front seat and hand them back to the baby one by one. Remember, you can't pick things up when he drops them, so it's recommended that you load up. By the end of the trip, your back-seat floor will look like the bottom of a claw machine.

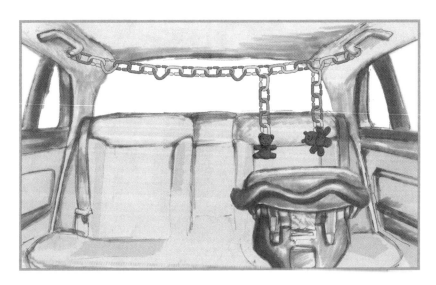

Tape photos onto a towel to keep your baby occupied in transit.

- Have a cup full of extra pacifiers in your cup holder.

- Create a playlist of your munchkin's favorite songs on the streaming app of your choice. If you need some inspiration, just search for "baby car songs," and a bunch of options will pop up. And if he starts to nod off, you can quickly switch to a "white noise" playlist (yes, they have those, too).

- Buy a bunch of plastic baby linking rings and create a chain across the grab handles above the rear windows. Hang soft toys from the links. Every time you pull over, you can take off old toys and put new ones on. Just make sure the chain doesn't obstruct your view, and that the toys are hung at a perfect height for a baby to reach out and bat them around. As an alternative, if your car seat is meant to be in the "carry" position during car rides (meaning the handle is upright), you can attach toys directly to the handle.

- Tape family pictures and black-and-white patterns to a sheet or towel (or directly to the upholstery if it's a rental) and secure it to the back of the seat in baby's view.

FYI: That weird smell in the car might be coming from a curdled milk bottle that rolled under the seat last month. Perform regular sweeps.

The Mirror Puppet Sing-Along

This little-known technique usually works when all else fails.

You will need three things:

- A soft hand puppet that you can wear without impairing your driving ability
- A mirror that clips onto the back seat
- A playlist of upbeat baby songs

Instructions

Place the puppet on your hand and make sure the baby can see it in his mirror. Get his attention by talking in a loud, obnoxious puppet voice. Press play and sing along, manipulating the puppet's mouth as you go. But always remember to keep your eyes on the road.

The people in cars on either side of you most likely won't be able to see the baby and may think you insane. But that's the price you pay for a happy little scamp.

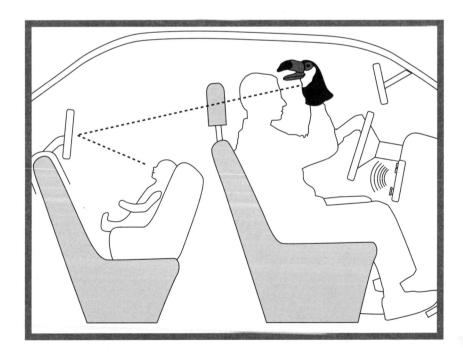

Using the Baby
as a
PROP

In a study cited by *Psychology Today*, men who were seen caring for babies were viewed as more attractive, kind, fatherly, and nurturing. As the article noted, this is probably the reason why politicians are always holding babies.

Why not take advantage of your newfound superpower? Whenever you need to negotiate with someone, bring the kid along for leverage.

When preparing the baby for the sting, make sure that he's bathed, changed, and fresh off a nap. Have your partner help pick out his wardrobe. Remember, you're going for maximum cuteness here.

Some Suggestions

Returning an Item Without a Receipt
For best results, place the baby in the car seat right up on the customer service counter. If you get any resistance, you can say that he may in fact have eaten the receipt, and you'll be glad to take off his diaper and look for it.

Jury Duty
Take your baby on a field trip and teach him the loopholes of the legal system at the same time. With a squirming baby in your lap, you'll be sent home faster than you can say "voir dire."

Getting "Bumped Up" in Long Lines
This one can go both ways. People may invite you to cut ahead of them if they see you with a baby, or they may just sneer and pretend they don't notice you. But if there's a full diaper involved, the odds are in your favor.

Meeting Potential Mates
If you happen to be a single dad, just walk around the mall and wait for the feeding frenzy. And if you are married, why not lend the baby out to a trustworthy single friend? Of course you should be there as backup, but don't walk alongside your buddy. People might assume that he's spoken for.

Buying a Car
Babies can melt the hearts of even the most jaded car dealer. Who could haggle with a face like that, especially when you tell the dealer that unless he lowers the price, your little genius will be forced to go to community preschool? They may just end up throwing in free rust-proofing.

Taking a Sick Day
Now that you have the baby, you have so many more excuses to play hooky from work. You're sick, the baby's sick, the babysitter never showed up, and so on. Give your boss the news via video chat with the sprout in your arms.

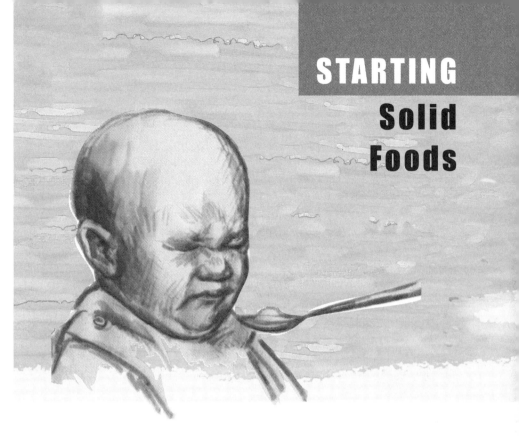

STARTING
Solid Foods

New fatherhood is full of memorable moments, but perhaps none will surpass the look on your baby's face as he takes his first spoonful of solid food. You can almost guarantee that no matter how bland the offering may be, your little drama king will react as if you have just given him a double shot of Jägermeister. Get your phones out, because that crazy face is definitely a moment you'll want to replay over and over.

Ironically, it's pretty much the same expression you'll exhibit upon opening up the first solid-food diaper. Now that the baby is starting to eat like one of us, he'll be evacuating like one of us as well. Suddenly you'll realize how good you had it those first few months.

Before introducing solids, note the following:

- Wait until your baby is around six months old, give or take. Very young babies have a tongue-thrust reflex that prevents them from choking, but also makes it nearly impossible to get solid food to the back of his throat. Also, young babies' intestin̄ɛ̄ ... ̇ ... ... p-
erly hold in nutrients and filter out h̄ ̇ ̄n̄ɨ̄ı̄ substances.

- If he is able to sit up in a high chair, lunges for your french fries, or pretends to chew when he sees you chewing, he's probably ready to start on solid foods.

- To make sure he doesn't have food allergies, some experts recommend introducing one food for a few consecutive days before moving on to the next one. If your baby has a reaction, like a rash, hives, or vomiting, you'll know which food is the culprit.

For Successful Solid-Food Delivery

No-Slip the Seat If your pollywog is slipping around in the high chair, cut a square piece of a bath mat and suction it onto the seat.

Contain the Mess If you don't have a dog, you'll need to find a way to clean up the splatter pattern your little goblin will leave on the floor. Buy a cheap shower curtain and place it under the high chair before meals. Or, if you want to try to make a few bucks, put a canvas down there and sell the results as an abstract masterpiece. Sign it "Snackson Pollock."

Never Force It These early feedings are more about the mealtime ritual than actually getting food down. The bulk of his nutrition and calories are still coming from milk or formula. So if he's not interested, try again tomorrow. The worst thing you can do is teach him to dread feeding time.

Feeder's Choice Some pediatricians used to recommend starting with vegetables, surmising that once the baby tastes the sugars in fruit, he won't settle for anything less. But that theory has been debunked. Basically any of the foods listed on the following page will do the trick.

Try a Naked Lunch Strip the baby down to his diaper before meals, and let him get as messy as he wants. When he's finished, just put him in the tub. Or better yet, feed him in the tub. Let him make his own soup.

A bath mat on the high chair will prevent sliding.

Open Sesame There are many ways to coerce your hatchling to open his mouth. Try getting him to smile by singing, making faces, or feeding him with the other end of the spoon clenched between your teeth. Also, if you open your mouth as you bring the spoon to his lips, he may imitate you. (Many dads start to do this unconsciously and continue through toddlerhood.)

Choose Your Spoon Wisely A baby spoon with a shallow trough is easier to use as a spackling tool, which is what you'll need as you continuously scrape the glop from his chin back into his mouth. And always have an extra spoon on hand to give the baby in case he tries to commandeer yours. There is a wide variety of spoons in the shape of airplanes, cartoon characters, sports logos, even spoons that change color when the food is too hot.

Solids Aren't Solid Start off with foods that are mashed, strained, or pureed, nothing that requires chewing, and the less lumpy the better. Your baby is already dealing with a whole new world of flavors and textures. You don't want to throw too much at him at once.

Some good choices for first foods

Rice cereal*	Beans and lentils
Oat cereal*	Yogurt
Barley cereal*	Applesauce
Sweet potato	Apricots
Peas	Bananas
Carrots	Peaches
Sweet peas	Prunes
Meats	Pears
Avocado	
Squash	*mix breast milk or formula into cereals*

Serve an Appetizer Time solid foods for when the baby is not too hungry or too full. If he's too hungry, he may have no tolerance, and if he's too full, he may be disinterested or sleepy. Offer a small amount of milk right before a round of solids.

Tongue Targets When serving fruits, aim for the front of the tongue, where the taste buds for sweetness are located. When serving vegetables, aim for the middle of the tongue, where the taste buds are neutral.

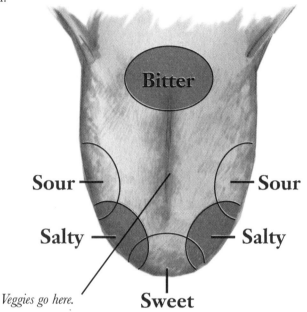

Bitter

Sour   Sour

Salty   Salty

Veggies go here.   **Sweet**

Baby-Led Weaning

We understand that baby-led *anything* sounds like a terrible idea, but baby-led weaning is a growing trend. Instead of going the traditional route of starting off with pureed and premade foods created specifically for babies, some parents choose to let the baby decide what— and when—to eat. When you sit down for a family meal, the baby is eating basically the same foods that you are, albeit cut up into tiny, bite-size pieces placed in front of him. And if he's not hungry, and just wants to play with his pile of caviar, that's totally fine.

Proponents of baby-led weaning say that it gives little ones agency to develop their own tastes and eating habits, helps them model eating behavior from their parents, and exposes them to a greater variety of foods. Should you want to delve further, there is plenty of info online.

CONSTIPATION

As he is starting solids, stool production may go down, but the density of each stool goes way up. Although it's best to have him making daily deposits, it's not uncommon for some ankle biters to go three or four days without an offering. And as long as your baby seems comfortable, that's not a problem. But if you see that he is straining really hard, is in obvious discomfort, or is passing dry, hard stools, then chances are he's constipated.

Here are a few ways to unplug the dam

1. **The Four P's** Prunes, plums, pears, and peaches, in either fruit or juice form, can have a laxative effect.

2. **Bicycle Legs** Lay the baby on his back. Holding his ankles, gently press one leg up against his chest, and then the other, creating a pedaling motion. This helps move things along.

3. **Bath Bomb** Place the baby in a warm bath. Make sure the water is up to around chest level. Now, while holding him steady with one hand, gently massage his abdomen with the other. In most cases, it won't take more than a minute or two for him to uncork, but it will take you much longer to clean him off and decontaminate the area.

4. **The ExerSaucer** Not only is the ExerSaucer a favorite toy for many babies this age, but the apparatus gives him a unique position from which to push, allowing his feet to be planted on the ground and his hands to brace against the rim. Although it doesn't have the same effect on every chunkard, dads the world over have noted the magical poop-inducing effects of the ExerSaucer.

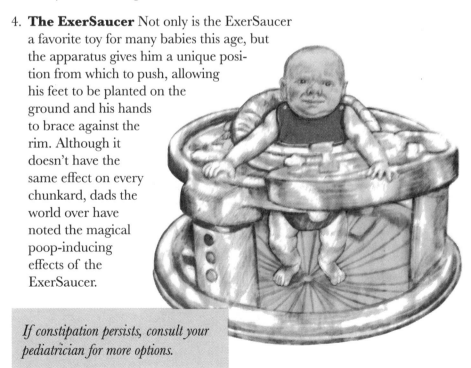

If constipation persists, consult your pediatrician for more options.

Effective Diaper Disposal

A few years back, if anyone had told you that you'd be collecting and storing human waste in your HOUSE for days on end, you'd dismiss them as bonkers. Yet here we are.

Because it's nearly impossible to run outside every time the baby fills a diaper, many parents rely on diaper disposal units. But the most popular brands are bulky and expensive, and some require special refills. And emptying the pail is a grisly process reminiscent of that scene in *Jaws* where they slice open the dead shark's belly and remove its innards.

And because plastic is gas permeable, it's almost impossible to efficiently hold in the smell. Like air slowly leaking out of a balloon, odor will eventually seep out into the atmosphere and create that distinctive "house-with-a-new-baby smell"—a combination of dirty diapers and a bunch of scents trying in vain to mask them.

As your chickadee gets older, and the waste becomes solid, you can dump it in the toilet, but until then, try implementing the process we call "The Bag and Drop." We suggest using biodegradable doggie bags. And you'll be saving the dump from another unwieldy diaper pail and all those refills.

The Bag

Step #1

Fold the soiled diaper into a ball and secure with the tabs

Step #2

Put your hand all the way inside the bag and use it to grab the diaper

Step #3

Pull your hand back through, so the diaper is now inside the bag

Step #4

Squeeze the air out of the bag, cinch it right above the diaper, and twist it around one rotation

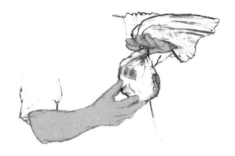

Step #5

Tie a knot in the bag. You now have some degree of odor protection. But remember, plastic is gas permeable, so we proceed to . . .

The Drop

Place one of your large outdoor trash cans under the window of the baby's room. (If you live in a city, you can hang a bag from the rail of your fire escape.) Each time you get a dirty diaper, simply open the window and shoot a long-range jumper. Once a day, you can go out and collect the air balls, but you'll be surprised how fast you'll get your rhythm down. At the end of the week when you take out the garbage, just bring the diaper can with it.

And if you use cloth diapers, more power to you, but you've got your own waste disposal issues to deal with.

The Claw

A Variation on the Arcade Crane Game

Four-to-six-month-olds are starting to grasp objects, and here's a fun way to sharpen their skills. Place a bunch of toys on the floor, and hold your tyke face down on your forearm (see illustration). Make robot noises as you move him into position. When he's hovering directly above the prizes, lower him onto the pile (bending from the knees), wait five seconds, and then slowly lift him up again. If he comes up with anything, shout, "We have a winner!"

This exercise builds hand-eye coordination, depth perception, and fine motor skills.

Flashlight Animal Theater

Lie down with baby in the crook of your arm and turn out the lights. Shine a flashlight on the wall. That alone will get his attention. Then, assuming you're not adept at hand shadows, get some flat animal shapes—pop-outs from the little foam books, the sticky bathtub shapes, refrigerator magnets, etc.—and put them in front of the flashlight. Move them closer, and the projected image becomes larger; farther away, and it gets smaller. Make appropriate animal noises.

This exercise builds visual discrimination, depth perception, and helps with language development.

Baby Balloonist

Tie a Mylar balloon very loosely to the baby's ankle. He will stare intently at the balloon for a while, and probably get excited. Excitement will lead to kicking, which, in turn, will cause the balloon to bob and jerk. Sooner or later, the baby will begin to understand and appreciate this cause-and-effect relationship.

For double the delight, tie a balloon to his wrist as well. Just make sure he doesn't float away.

This exercise builds foot-eye coordination, reasoning skills, and body awareness.

Always supervise the baby during this exercise. And never use rubber or latex balloons, because if they pop, the little bits of rubber can be choking hazards.

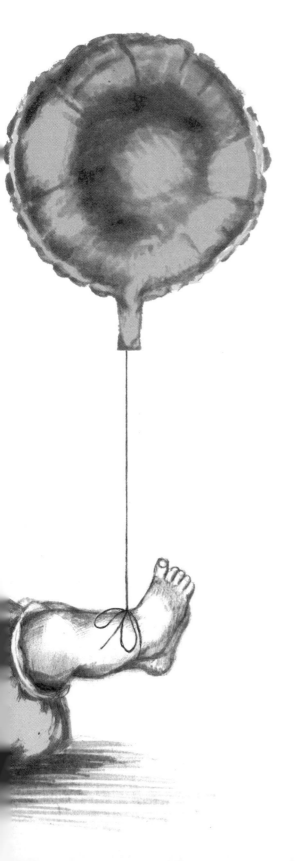

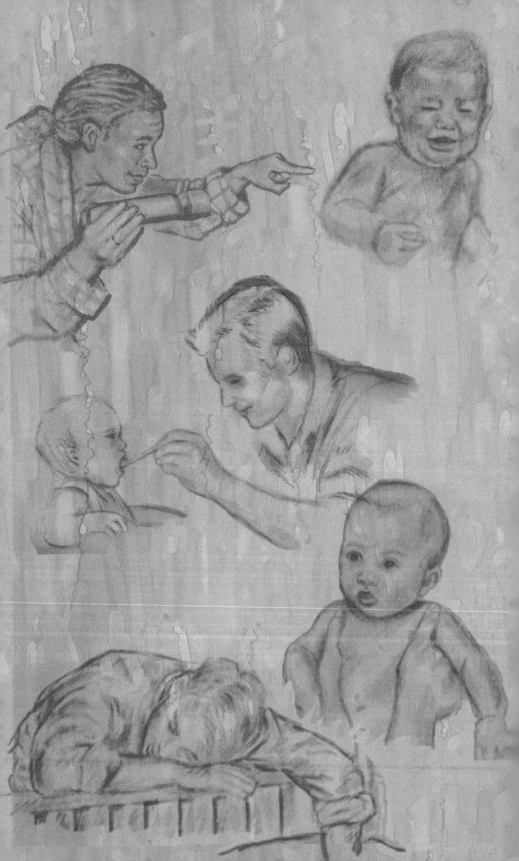

7–9 MONTHS

Sleeping
Through the Night

Your baby can now sleep in her own room. She has been steadily gaining weight, and her stomach capacity is growing. This means feedings don't need to be as frequent. And when she does wake up in the middle of the night (as we all do), she's developing the ability to self-soothe. So finally, you and your partner will be able to get a full night's sleep, right?

Not necessarily. While a few tots start sleeping through the night at four months old, others keep their parents on retainer well after their first birthday. As you've probably noticed by now, babies are all over the map. A 2018 study revealed that 57% of six-month-olds were not sleeping through the night. (By the way, "sleeping through the night" means six to eight straight hours uninterrupted.)

Here are three tactics for helping your little insomniac get to sleep and stay asleep.

Become a Drill Sergeant

If you go to a workplace during the day and your partner is home, you'll likely take charge of the bedtime routine. This gives you valuable baby bonding time while affording your partner a well-deserved respite. After being away from the baby for eight hours, your instinct may be to rile her up with some impromptu baby wrestling. But as bedtime approaches, the goal is to foster a serene environment conducive to sleep, so you might have to cool your jets.

Baby bedtime can still be fun in a mellow, Mr. Rogers-like sense. When presiding over the nighttime shift, keep in mind:

- The activities you choose should be soothing
- Do them in the same order every night
- You progress from least- to most-sleep-inducing activities (so you wouldn't go right from the bathtub into the crib)

Remember that babies, like senior citizens, thrive on routine. They take comfort in repetitive daily patterns, and will usually put up less resistance if they know what's expected of them.

Example of a nighttime routine:
1. Bath or wipe down
2. Diaper change
3. Put on pajamas
4. Say goodnight to all the people and objects in the room
5. Turn on lullaby music mix
6. Bottle-feed
7. Read a bedtime story
8. Sing a lullaby while rocking her

Create a Field of Pacifiers

If your baby uses a pacifier to sleep, odds are it falls out in the middle of the night and she wakes up trying to find it. To solve this problem,

liberally sprinkle pacifiers around the perimeter of the crib. Don't put them right next to her, because she may roll over on one and awaken. But if you place them around the outside, she'll eventually discover that they are always at arm's length.

If you have fewer than six pacifiers in your home, you are asking for trouble. Pacifiers rival socks and umbrellas for the title of "Items That Vanish into Thin Air Most Often." If you can buy them in bulk, do so. You won't regret it.

Fill 'er Up

About fifteen to twenty minutes before bed, load up the baby with as much milk as she can hold. If she gets drowsy mid-feed, don't be afraid to gently jostle her to see if you can top her off. Those extra few ounces may just buy you a couple of extra hours of slumber. But try to follow it up with a quick tooth cleaning or a sip of water to rinse out the milk before she falls off.

"Feeding your baby to sleep" is when you put her to bed by feeding her until she's out. Experts warn against this practice, because babies this age can start to rely on it as a sleep aid.

How to Deal with 4 a.m. Wake-Ups

When your fuss monster's cry wakes you up from a sound sleep, what do you do? If you're like most dads, you'll pretend not to hear it, hoping that your partner will respond. Your partner is no doubt employing the same tactic. And believe it or not, both of you are doing the right thing. The best way to deal with a crying seven-to-nine-month-old in the middle of the night is to wait and see if she can self-soothe and fall back to sleep on her own.

Oddly enough, babies often practice their developing skills half asleep in their cribs. You may see your little gymnast rocking back and forth on her hands and knees or rolling around semiconscious. It's like Cirque du Bébé in there. She may yelp, grunt, whimper, and eventually nod off again. So before you go in, wait a minute or two. (Obviously, if it's a pain or distress cry, enter immediately.)

When you do go in:

- Keep the lights low. If she doesn't sleep with a night light, install a dim red bulb in a table lamp so you won't trip over her paraphernalia.

  - Don't smile or frown, and make as little eye contact as possible. Try to be monotonous, which shouldn't be hard under the circumstances.

  - If she wakes demanding a bottle, it could be simply out of habit. Try giving her a bottle with some water in it to see if that does the trick. After a few nights, she may lose interest.

Sleep training is a way of teaching your baby to self-soothe and fall asleep on her own. It's not for the faint of heart, because it involves letting her cry in her crib for extended periods of time while you wait out in the hallway trying your best not to have a panic attack. Many parents swear by this method, claiming that it helped their baby—and themselves— sleep through the night.

Although she will probably cry harder than you ever thought possible (sometimes so hard that she'll vomit), pediatricians assure that no long-term emotional harm will be done to your little angel. You, on the other hand, may experience flashbacks for decades.

Babies aren't ready for sleep training until at least 4–6 months of age. Many parents wait even longer, while others make the choice to not sleep train at all. Before you start, it's important that you and your partner are both committed to the process. You are likely to be elected official sleep trainer, especially if your partner is breastfeeding, as all that crying can trigger her milk flow.

Online, you can find a wide variety of sleep-training methods. Below are three of the most common:

The Ferber Method

Developed by Dr. Richard Ferber, this method has you leaving the room with the baby still awake in the crib. She will most likely start crying. If she's still crying after three minutes, go back in and put your hand on her chest or talk softly to her for about thirty seconds, reassuring her that you're not her dad's evil twin. But don't pick her up. Leave the room again, and this time wait five minutes before coming back. Increase the intervals between check-ins until you hit ten minutes. Over subsequent nights, further increase the intervals, until, after about a week, she should be sleep trained.

The Cry-It-Out Method

This is similar to the Ferber method except you never come back. After you put her into the crib, you hightail it out of the room and lie down in the hallway in the fetal position until she cries herself to sleep. Proponents of this method claim it works the fastest, and critics worry about possible long-term emotional effects.

The Chair Method

You leave the room, and when the baby starts to cry, you come back and silently sit in a chair next to the crib. Don't engage with her. Just sit there until she falls asleep. The next night, you move the chair a few feet farther away from the crib. Repeat every night until the baby falls asleep without fussing, or the chair is in the next town over.

Once your baby is sleep trained, don't assume she will stay that way. Sleep training can become derailed by illness, teething, or visiting grandparents who insist on rocking her to sleep every night. If she regresses, it will take some time to get her back on schedule.

Transitional OBJECTS

Your kiddo may start to form an emotional attachment to an inanimate object, keeping it close by at all times. Her obsession with this "transitional object" is generally regarded as a healthy one, and provides fringe benefits for the whole family. Because holding her new pal gives her comfort and reassurance, you have yet another tool for soothing her when she gets upset. The phrase "security blanket" was born from this very idea.

And though many babies choose an actual blanket, others may form an attachment to a stuffed animal, burp cloth, oven mitt, drumstick, plastic bowl, toothbrush, or one of your T-shirts. The heart wants what it wants. (Just make sure the item is baby-safe.)

Some things to keep in mind:

- Steer her toward something that is easily replaceable, like an Elmo doll, rather than a hard-to-find item, like a match-worn Lionel Messi jersey. And buy multiples.

- Always bring one (or three) with you when you are traveling. Being in an unfamiliar environment can overwhelm her.

- When you and your partner leave her with a relative or babysitter, the object can alleviate separation anxiety.

- The item can go with her everywhere except the crib, which needs to remain free of potential hazards.

- If your little one hasn't organically formed a bond with an item, there's no need to worry. Only about 60% of babies do.

If she gets attached to an object, buy extras.

Going Mobile

Your baby's first crawl is a proud moment for a new dad. Suddenly, she's in control of her own destiny and can go wherever she wants. Congratulations, you've got a self-driving baby.

But that drive isn't always smooth. While many mites adopt the traditional crawl, plenty of others find their own, often unorthodox methods of locomotion. Some slither on their bellies, others shuffle on their butts, and still others simply roll from place to place. If you have one of these rogue crawlers, don't worry. It's not the method that's important, it's the fact that she's learning to get around that matters.

Most babies learn to crawl between six and ten months, and usually by a year almost all are at least somewhat mobile. If your baby props herself up on her hands and knees and rocks back and forth, she's ready for takeoff. You can assist by:

- modeling a crawl for her
- letting her feet push against your hands, propelling her forward
- putting a favorite toy just out of her reach
- protecting her knees from hard floors and rug burns by cutting the toe area off a pair of your old socks and sticking them over her legs

And once she's got the basics down, create an obstacle course made up of couch cushions, throw pillows, and empty shoeboxes to improve her agility and maneuverability.

Advanced crawlers have been clocked at speeds of up to two miles per hour and can cover 200 yards in a single day (your mileage may vary).

Yet another use for your old socks: baby kneepads

Your baby may use any number of transportation methods

The Commando

slithering on stomach using elbows and knees to propel forward

The Naked Ape

walking forward on hands and feet, rear lifted off the ground

The Sit 'n' Slide

from a seated position, using hands to drive rear end forward

The Low Roller

lying down and rolling from place to place, picking up crumbs and dust balls along the way

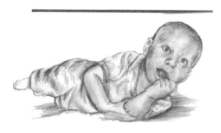

The Jackknife

one leg shooting out to the side, and the other remaining under her (baby tends to go in circles)

Babyproofing

Tots are drawn to faces. Whoever designed the outlet was clearly a psychopath.

Sadly, your mobile munchkin does not come with any built-in safety features. If anything, it seems like she's bent on self-destruction. If there is a staircase, she will attempt to fling herself down it; if there is an outlet, she will try to stick something into it; and if there's an inch of water anywhere, she will try to lie in it, face down. It's like she's auditioning for *Baby Jackass*.

It's time to get out the toolbox and start proofing!

1. Secure a pad, a pencil, and a flashlight;

2. Get down on your hands and knees; and

3. Crawl around every room, taking note of all the ways you could possibly injure yourself.

Don't be lazy. Scurry under tables and behind drapes, and you'll be surprised at all the hazards you'll find, like exposed nails, loose change, and latches that could close on your baby's little sausage fingers.

If you're not the hands-and-knees type, and you've got some extra cash on hand, you can always pay a professional baby-proofer to do the job for you. But be warned: you'll likely be told that your house is a giant death trap, and that your runt doesn't stand a chance unless you purchase a wide array of devices that just happen to be in the babyproofer's trunk.

Keep in mind that there is such a thing as too much babyproofing. If you turn your entire home into a giant playpen, your baby will have trouble learning self-control, especially when you take her to other people's homes or stores.

And the truth is that no matter how many gizmos you install, you should still NEVER LEAVE YOUR BABY UNATTENDED. The day you let your guard down is the day she tries to eat the little plastic tip off the door stopper. (You need to glue it on or buy a one-piece stopper.)

Grab a flashlight and search all the nooks and crannies in your home.

How Many Ways Can Your Baby Injure Herself in the...

The baby could:

Crawl into fireplace. *Install fireplace screen.*

Knock fire tools on top of herself or try to suck on them. *Place out of reach.*

Fall on edges of glass table. *Place rubber protectors around all edges.*

Try to eat candy in dish. *Place out of reach.*

Pull sculpture on top of herself. *Place out of reach.*

Eat dirt from potted plant. *Put netting over it.*

Eat the plant, which may be poisonous. *Keep out of reach, and know the names of all houseplants and which are poisonous.*

Mash a Cheerio into the disc slot of the game console. *Move it up and out of reach.*

Can you find at least 18 hazards?

Living Room?

Bang her head on the sharp edges of the square tables. *Get corner guards.*

Topple over the speakers. *Put them out of reach or bolt them down.*

Walk into sliding glass doors face-first. *Put decals on doors.*

Pull bookcase down on herself. *Add furniture anchors.*

Tangle herself in drape cords. *Wrap them so they're out of reach.*

Knock over wineglass and cut herself on broken shards. *Place out of reach.*

Knock over standing lamp. *Fasten to wall.*

Tangle herself in lamp's electrical cord. *Wrap cord.*

Shove something into outlet. *Get outlet covers.*

Fall and smack her head on hearth. *Install a padded cushion around hearth.*

How Many Ways Can Your Baby **Injure** Herself in the . .

The baby could:

Reach up to the counter and spill hot coffee on herself. *Move out of reach.*

Reach up and touch front burner or knock the pot down on herself. *Always use back burners and turn pot handles inward.*

Twist knobs and turn on gas. *Install shield or knob covers.*

Pull open the stove door. *Install appliance latch.*

Open cabinet under sink and get at cleaning products. *Install lock on cabinet.*

Choke on refrigerator magnets. *Remove them, because even if you put them high up, they tend to fall.*

Tip the foreground chair onto herself. *Push in all chairs.*

Eat contents of trash can. *Put in locked cabinet.*

154

Kitchen?

Pull down tablecloth and send bowl and glass on top of herself. *Always use placemats instead.*

Grab the knife off of the counter and run around like a Chucky doll. *Move out of reach.*

Open dishwasher and take out contents or try to eat detergent. *Install shield.*

Eat kibble from dog's food bowl or put head into water bowl. *Keep in separate gated area. (And do the same with litter boxes, which, to babies, look like sandboxes.)*

Because the kitchen is probably the hardest place to keep babyproofed, you can always put up a safety gate in the doorway to bar entry completely.

155

The baby could:

Close bathroom door on her fingers. *Place a towel over the door or buy finger-pinch guards.*

Press doorknob button, locking herself in bathroom. *Install a knob cover over doorknob.*

Open toilet lid and fall into bowl. *Install a lid lock on the toilet.*

Open cabinet under the sink and get at the contents. *Install a cabinet lock.*

Eat the toothpaste, which can be poisonous to small children. *Place out of reach.*

Knock hair dryer into sink or toilet, or tangle self in cord. *Place out of reach.*

Bathroom?

Slip and fall right outside of tub. *Install no-slip bath rug. (Also, install rubber bath mat inside tub.)*

Bang head into tub faucet. *Install faucet shield.*

Turn knobs, releasing scalding water. *Install knob covers, turn down water heater below 120°F, or install a scald guard.*

Try to eat razor and shampoo on the edge of the tub. *Install a rack that is placed out of reach.*

Drown in small amount of water left in tub. *Always drain water.*

To keep your baby out of the bathroom entirely, you can install a latch high up on the outside of the door.

BUT WAIT, There's More

The Home Office

- Bolt down your monitor to prevent the baby genius from pulling it on top of herself.

- Thread all of your cords through a tube so she won't use them as teethers.

- Get a surge protector cover. Babies love little red lights.

- Anchor all bookcases to the wall.

- If you have a PC tower, use a computer guard to prevent her from shutting your computer down before you've had a chance to save your thesis.

- Office trash cans with staples and paper clips need to be either lockable or placed out of reach of your little dumpster diver.

This is the actual size of the hole in a toilet paper tube (1½ inches). Use it for reference if you don't have a real tube handy.

Toys

- Make sure that all toys are baby-safe, with no small pieces that could break off.

- Check the eyes of stuffed animals to see if they can be easily chewed off.

- If you think something may be too small for the little lass to play with, use a toilet paper tube as a toy tester. If the toy fits through the tube, the baby could choke on it. (And don't let her play with the toilet paper tube. She could bite off chunks.)

Dads and Gates

Much of your time at home will be spent hurdling baby gates. Every doorbell ring is like a starting gun at the Olympics. Just remember to use extra care when negotiating these barriers, especially when you're carrying the baby. Almost every dad has a story about misjudging a gate and narrowly avoiding an impromptu vasectomy.

General Safety

- If your home or apartment was built before 1978, check it for lead paint using a testing kit.

- Install smoke alarms, CO_2 detectors and fire extinguishers throughout your home, and escape ladders for second-floor windows.

- Cover all radiators to prevent burns.

- Install guards on all windows above the first floor.

- Set your water heater to 120°F maximum to prevent burns.

- Have all emergency phone numbers, especially the Poison Control Hotline, easily accessible, and take an infant first-aid and CPR class.

- Keep all poisonous substances, like cleaning products and laundry detergents, out of reach at all times. As we all know, kids can't resist eating Tide pods.

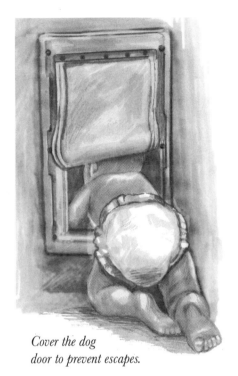

Cover the dog door to prevent escapes.

Getting Her Steps In

Gates should be installed at the top and bottom of all staircases. But every once in a while, remove the bottom gate and let your little mountaineer try to climb up the first few steps with you holding on to her. (You'll want carpeting or a runner on the staircase to prevent slippage.) This is great exercise, and eventually she'll start to get the hang of this exciting new technology. Climbing down the stairs, however, is much more treacherous. It requires the "butt first" approach, which is contradictory to her go-big-or-go-home instincts. Save that for when she's older.

THE MEAN SCREEN?

Is it okay to plop your piglet in front of a video? This is a tricky question, and much of it depends on who you ask. But the overwhelming consensus is—the less time the better.

The American Academy of Pediatrics recommends minimal or no screen time before the age of 18 months, with the exception of interactive video chatting. This hard-line stance is based on studies revealing that babies learn best when you interact with them, with facial expressions, movement, touch, and other external stimuli. And while many little ones are fascinated by screens, they struggle to bridge the gap between two-dimensional images and tangible experiences. In other words, ditch the screens and stick to IRL.

Yet many parents admit to using a small amount of screen time as part of their babycare routine. A recent survey revealed that 92% have showed their tots content on a tablet or phone before the age of one. Are these parents monsters, or do they just want to take a quick shower in peace?

Of course, screens are no substitute for reading, playing, singing, or a stroll in the park, and we definitely don't recommend throwing the baby in front of the TV and heading to Vegas for the weekend. But used sparingly, they can be an enjoyable diversion. After several hours of high-energy, in-your-face dad-baby interaction, how much harm could twenty minutes of passive staring do?

And what about your emotional state? If you've been with Fussy McGee all day and need to unwind, decompress, maybe pay a bill, answer an email, or make dinner, it's better to put the baby in front of a screen than for you to become impatient or resentful. Studies have shown babies can pick up on anger in their caretakers and, over time, start to feel unsafe.

So strap her into a bouncy seat, throw on a baby video, and twenty minutes later, you'll come back rejuvenated and ready for fifty more verses of "Old MacDonald."

Baby Sensory Videos

An avocado in a sombrero dances to a beat while fluffy clouds drip smiling raindrops, and a rainbow octopus spins and laughs. No, you haven't been dosed with ayahuasca. You're watching a baby sensory video.

Baby sensory videos combine high-contrast colors, shapes and patterns, happy music, and gentle movements designed to captivate the baby brain. Proponents claim that the videos can be watched by tykes as young as three months of age, and that they can "stimulate eyesight" and "enhance focus." There is no proof that they are educational, but babies seem to really enjoy them. Some of the most popular have hundreds of millions of views on YouTube. (Keep in mind that some of those clicks are from stoners.)

Video Chatting (It's Not Just for Pandemics)

The American Academy of Pediatrics gives a thumbs-up on video chatting, with one caveat—that you try to keep it interactive. Here are a few tips on creating a lively back-and-forth.

1. Help the conversation come alive. If the person on-screen waves at the baby, help her wave back. If they blow her a kiss, plant one on her cheek.

2. Send the person a copy of one of baby's favorite books, and have them read to her while you follow along and turn the pages.

3. Sing a song together and clap along.

4. Feed the baby during the call, and offer a spoon up to the screen, imploring the person to open wide.

5. Since elderly relatives often have a hard time adjusting their cameras, turn it into an impromptu game of peek-a-boo. "Where's Grandma? I see her neck. Now I see the top of her head. Where could she be?!"

Your whippersnapper is becoming highly social and wants to be included in your interactions with others. She's also entering the perpetual-motion stage. Outings for babies at this stage include:

Racetrack

A stimulating trip for both dad and baby. You can cheer your picks, visit the horses in the paddock, and rip up your tickets and have her help you throw them in the air. It's best to go on an off day, so you can get a good view of the action without having to fight the crowds. And who knows? She just may be a better handicapper than you are.

Bookstore

Yes, they still exist! A bookstore is a great place for babies because it's just like a library, but you don't have to be quiet. Many are carpeted, so beginning crawlers can scoot through the aisles, and some even have snacks. (Oh, and they have books, too.)

Car Wash

The rushing water and spinning brushes of the car wash can provide a great sensory experience for your oompa loompa. Before you enter, give her cues that this is going to be a safe, fun experience for the both of you. "Look—the car is taking a bath!"

Laundromat

Even if you have a washing machine at home, bring a load down to the local laundromat just so you and your progeny can sit and watch the clothes dance through that little window. She can help throw everything in and take it out. Then put her in the laundry cart, hang a sheet from the top bar, and pretend she's sailing the seven seas (while maintaining a firm grip, of course).

Dog Park

While we definitely don't recommend going inside a dog park, standing right outside the fence can provide a delightful experience for your tot. Some dog parks have special areas for small dogs, where you may be able to safely enter and watch all of the pint-size action up close. It's also a great way for her to learn that everybody poops.

Aquarium

If you are lucky enough to live near an aquarium, taking your moppet is a must. You'll see a wide array of amazing, colorful creatures just inches away from your face. And even though the sharks may look at your baby like a Lunchable, it's comforting to know there are two inches of glass separating you.

Three-Cup Monte

This is a baby-friendly version of the old street scam. Start off
with three large cups and a ball or small stuffed animal. You're
the "operator," and the baby is your "mark." Lift all of the cups
so she can see where the object is, and then lower them all. If she
chooses the right cup, she wins. And when she starts becoming
consistent, slowly jockey the cups around.

*Builds visual memory, problem-solving skills, and helps develop the concept of
object permanence—the fact that objects exist even when she can't see them.*

Suction Magic

Looking for a way to play and clean at the same time? Have butterfingers drop a bunch of Cheerios around the room, and then magically suck them up with the vacuum cleaner, along with all the other crumbs and dust. Note that the sound of the vacuum is basically white noise, so this game may be interrupted by a power nap.

Builds hand-eye coordination, spatial awareness, and baby's sense of wonder.

The Culinary Arts

Encourage pookie's burgeoning artistic skills and introduce her to a few new foods at the same time. Fill several plastic containers with baby foods of different colors. Put them in front of her and encourage her to finger paint the tray of her high chair or the kitchen table. (You may need to demo for her.) Some good colorful foods to use are sweet potatoes, prunes, green beans, and, for texture, rice cereal. She can create an abstract masterpiece and safely eat the results. (You can also try four bowls of mashed potatoes and some baby-safe food coloring.)

This activity is best done right before bath time.

Builds creativity, fine motor skills, and hand-eye coordination.

The Basket Train

Sit the cherub in a laundry basket with a blanket or pillow against her back. Fill the rest of the basket with stuffed animals and toys, and push it around the house, simulating train noises. At various points along the way, announce stops where you drop off and pick up creatures. Eventually, she will anticipate each stop where she can throw some animals out and invite others on board. This game takes no small degree of exertion on your part, but the baby's enthusiasm will (hopefully) energize you.

To save on back strain, you can attach a rope or leash to the basket and slowly pull her around.

Builds sequential thinking and role-playing skills.

Babies and Language

Your baby may call all men "dada" for a while. No need to order a paternity test.

Have you noticed that your baby seems more interested in what you have to say these days? A couple of months ago, your explanation of the infield fly rule was met with a blank stare. But now the thick fog behind her eyes is starting to dissipate, giving way to a wonderfully perplexed expression. She's attempting to unravel the mysteries of language, and you are lucky enough to be able to shepherd her through this amazing and often hilarious journey.

On average, babies say their first words somewhere between 9 and 12 months, but this can vary widely. Your little scamp has probably started babbling, and may have even said "dada," much to your partner's chagrin. Don't tell your partner this, but "dada" is one of the most common babbling syllable combos, and is just as likely to be directed at the family dog as your face. In order for it to be considered a true first word, it needs to be said with intentionality.

vacuum

dog

truck

record

pickle

funny glasses

So unless she's said "dada" consistently while looking at you or your picture, it's not official. And don't be alarmed if she soon starts to refer to all men, or even all people, as "dada." Babies tend to learn in categories. She might also start calling all animals "doggy."

Babies can understand language much earlier than they're able to speak it effectively. This makes sense, as they've been watching and hearing you talk from birth. Also, their speech apparatus, as well as the brain's speech center, is still a work in progress. In the following sections you'll find a few ways to encourage language development.

Spark Dialogue

When you hear her babbling, join in as if you know what she is talking about. After she finishes a spurt of random syllables, say, "Yeeees, that's true, but how will that affect the overseas markets?" And then wait for a response. Pretty soon she'll start to figure out the back-and-forth nature of true conversation. Remember to always praise her utterances, no matter how economically unsound.

Label Everything

As an everyday ritual, walk around the house with your bundle of joy, naming everything as you go. You can use it as a passive-aggressive exercise. "See? This is a guitar. Gui-TAR. Daddy used to play this guitar every day, before you came along. And this is a basketball. BAS-ket-ball. Daddy used to ball all the time, before you came along." As long as you keep smiling, the imp will be none the wiser.

When naming things, try not to be too general or specific. A guitar is a guitar, not an instrument (too general) or a Fender Stratocaster (too specific).

Rhyme It

Research has shown that simple rhythm and rhyme is one of the best ways for children to learn language. Try reciting some Mother Goose standards, emphasizing and elongating the rhyming words. When you get bored, switch to hip-hop anthems.

Applaud All Sounds

When she points to the dog and says "dada," act very excited. She's starting to pair words with objects, a milestone that should be encouraged. Say, "Yes, that's a doggy! Doggy. Great job!" (Putting a -y on the end of words can make them easier for babies to distinguish and eventually sound out.)

Chew on Some Books

Interactive books, such as lift-the-flap books, books with zippers and buttons, and touch-and-feel books, not only build her vocabulary but also help with hand-eye coordination and fine motor skills.

And remember, there's no wrong way to read with a baby. As long as she is enjoying herself, it doesn't matter if she wants to read the same book over and over, flip each page back and forth a hundred times, or chew on one book as you're reading another. Just relax and take comfort in the fact that she's getting a taste for literature.

Here's a surefire way to spark your baby's book-loving instincts. Take one of your copies of *Goodnight Moon* (you'll no doubt be receiving multiples), cut out pictures of various family members, and tape them into the book. Then alter the words appropriately. "Goodnight house, and goodnight mouse, and goodnight Papa Neil, and goodnight Grandpa George."

The Secret Meaning
of Peek-a-Boo

Your baby's mind works in strange and screwy ways. Would you believe that whenever you step out of her field of vision, she thinks that you no longer exist? It's true. And for some reason, she isn't bothered by this. She just goes on playing or snacking or staring into space until you miraculously reappear. Every toy she drops, every pacifier she throws, and every loved one who wanders out of view ceases to exist as far as she is concerned.

But now she's starting to grasp the concept of object permanence—the idea that objects continue to endure even when she can't see them. Dads can help reinforce this skill by:

- playing peek-a-boo
- hiding a toy under a napkin and letting her unveil it
- showing her the object she just dropped on the ground before picking it up

Object permanence is a double-edged sword. As soon as she realizes that you are always somewhere, and that you can always be reached, she'll start to become nervous the minute you leave the room.

When you play peek-a-boo with babies, they think that your head literally disappears and then suddenly reappears when you open your hands. No wonder they are so impressed.

Dealing with Baby Anxiety

Why shouldn't your baby have anxiety just like the rest of us? With the onset of object permanence comes **separation anxiety**, the fear of separation from you or your partner, no matter who you leave the baby with, and **stranger anxiety**, the fear of strangers. Suddenly, everyone except you and your partner becomes a menacing interloper.

Some ways to deal with an anxious elf:

- Have visitors, including close relatives, approach the baby slowly, quietly, and with no sudden movements, the way you would advance toward an unexploded bomb or a rabid raccoon.

- If you are introducing a new babysitter or daycare situation, stay with the baby for at least the first couple of visits, and let her see you hanging out with the caretakers.

- Babies, like dogs, have no sense of time. For your first couple of outings, come back after fifteen or twenty minutes, just to let her know that you're not fleeing the country.

- Never sneak out on your baby. You'll just reinforce the anxiety. Instead, look her in the eye, smile, and act as if it's no big deal. And NEVER go back right in after you've left. Call home ten minutes later to make sure she stopped crying.

Believe it or not, the development of separation and stranger anxiety is a good thing. It means that you are doing your job as a dad. Your baby turns to you for safety and protection.

The Big Bath

As soon as your hatchling has trouble fitting in her infant tub and can sit up on her own, it's time to upgrade to the extra-roomy adult bathtub. Though she may resist at first, you can help her adjust. Don't add water for the first couple of baths. Climb in with a bunch of toys and act like you're having a blast.

Once she gets comfortable in the tub, chances are she won't want to leave. The prepared dad can use this to his advantage. It's an optimal place to feed her, give her medicine, and cut her nails. Pretty much anything you can do on dry land you can do in the tub, with better slop control.

Prepping for the Big Bath

1. Install a bath mat to prevent slippage.

2. Buy or make a spout cover, so she won't whack her head on the metal spout. You can create one by cutting six inches off a pool noodle and sticking it over the spout.

3. Fill up the tub with three to four inches of water. Remember, babies like baths almost as warm as adults do. Use the elbow test to make sure the temperature's right.

4. Because you need to be watching her at all times, be sure to have all of your supplies by your side, including a large plastic cup, baby soap and shampoo, a washcloth, and a towel.

Jumping In

There's no better time to play with your baby than when taking a bath together. Why sit hunched over the tub holding on to her when there's fun to be had right inside? Not only will she be enthralled by your demonstration of fluid dynamics, but she'll feel more comfortable and secure with you in the tub together.

Before you get your feet wet, be sure that you're prepared for:

Getting Her into and out of the Tub The safest way to enter and exit is to put her on a towel on top of a curved changing pad on the floor, get in the tub by yourself, sit down, and then bring her in with you. When exiting, put the baby back on the changing pad, get out by yourself, and then pick her up.

The Mid-bath Movement
At some point, your little dipper is likely to drop a load in the big bathtub. Think of it as her version of the New Year's Eve ball drop. In anticipation of this event, have a second large cup on hand to scoop up the scat as quickly as possible so you won't have to empty the tub and start over.

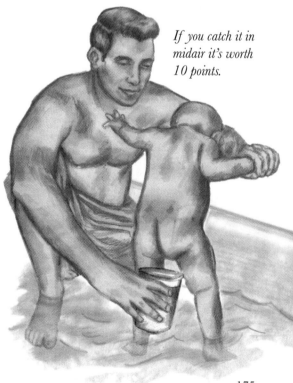

If you catch it in midair it's worth 10 points.

You'll know she's ready to launch when her body suddenly tenses up, her face turns red, and she grimaces.

Rinsing Out the Hair To avoid getting soap in her eyes when you rinse her hair, stick a suction cup toy to your forehead. While she tilts her head back to look at the odd spectacle, rinse from front to back. If your forehead won't hold a suction cup, putting a toy in your mouth and grunting may achieve similar results.

And if your baby has a high tolerance for headgear, you can buy a baby bath visor.

For the Landlubbers

If you'd prefer to be dry during the bath-time routine, your peanut will need some support to stay upright. Below are a few apparatuses that will help you out. (But remember, you still can never leave her in the bath unattended.)

Inflatable Tub It's a small tub that fits inside of your bathtub. It supports the baby's back and requires less water than the big tub. Also, bath toys stay within reach.

Bath Seat Held in place with suction cups, bath seats help keep her in place while providing you access to wash her body.

Laundry Basket Place a plastic laundry basket in the tub with a washcloth in the bottom to keep her from slipping. The basket supports her back, and water flows freely through the holes. Toys stay within reach, and when you are done, just drain the tub and store the toys in the basket.

A bath seat can hold the baby upright and in place.

Tub Toys

The resourceful dad needn't go out and buy bath toys. Anything in the house that floats (or sinks, for that matter) has potential.

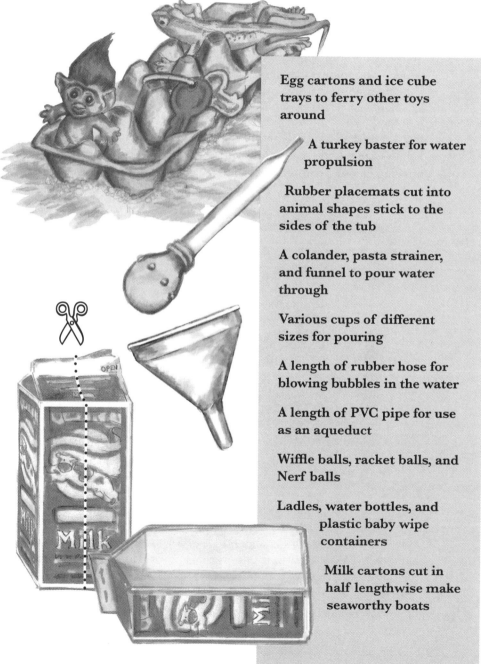

Egg cartons and ice cube trays to ferry other toys around

A turkey baster for water propulsion

Rubber placemats cut into animal shapes stick to the sides of the tub

A colander, pasta strainer, and funnel to pour water through

Various cups of different sizes for pouring

A length of rubber hose for blowing bubbles in the water

A length of PVC pipe for use as an aqueduct

Wiffle balls, racket balls, and Nerf balls

Ladles, water bottles, and plastic baby wipe containers

Milk cartons cut in half lengthwise make seaworthy boats

First Haircut

The only real reason to give a baby a haircut during the first year is maintenance—either the bangs are interfering with her vision or she's growing a mullet. In either case, action must be taken.

Your partner may suggest one of the many child-friendly styling salons—with names like ShortCutz, Clips'n'Giggles, or Hairy Potter's. But if you want to save some time and money, and possibly alleviate a tantrum, do it yourself.

If you are at all apprehensive at the prospect of cutting your baby's hair, realize that no matter how badly you botch the job (short of drawing blood), your baby will still look cute.

Cutting the Back

Place your baby in her high chair in front of the TV. (If you don't let her watch TV, your partner can provide a distraction.) Stand behind the baby, and using your rounded scissors, cut from the center out in both directions. Snip small amounts at a time so you can easily cover up errors. If all goes well, your youngster will be none the wiser.

Cutting the Bangs

Because babies will often whip their heads around to dodge approaching blades (a very good instinct in most situations), it's best to cut a baby's bangs when they are catnapping in the stroller or car seat, sitting upright enough for you to get a good angle. Use the round-edged scissors, and always have your fingers in between the scissors and the baby's head (see below).

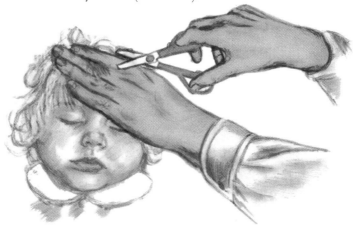

Nail Care

Babies don't have great control over their arms and legs, resulting in a lot of flailing around. And if they've got razor-sharp wolverine claws, they can easily scratch their face and yours. Unless you want them to wear mittens their whole lives, you've got to bite the bullet and cut their nails. And even if you've never had a mani-pedi, it's pretty easy once you get the hang of it.

If she's a heavy sleeper, you can do it then. Otherwise, you'll either need an assistant to hold her hand still or a very engaging distraction to keep her busy. Some dads do it right after a bath, when the nails are especially pliable.

Use a pair of baby nail clippers or scissors, or blunt-edged nose hair scissors, which some dads say are even easier to maneuver. To minimize the chance of catching skin, press the fleshy part of the finger down as you cut. And don't worry if you draw a tiny bit of blood. It happens to everybody, especially the first few times out with a fidgety baby. Just apply a sterile gauze pad.

10–12 MONTHS

EATING Like a Person (A Very Messy Person)

When you started your baby on solids, did you stop and think about how unsolid those foods were? Everything is pretty much the same consistency—mush. Well, by 10–12 months many babies rebel against the mush and start craving finger foods more and more. They look at the various shades of brownish slop on their plate, and then the burger and fries on yours, and you can't blame them for trying to fling themselves out of their high chairs in protest.

Not to mention the fact that the store-bought baby foods created for the ten- to twelve-month-old set are suspect, to say the least. Would you eat a jar of orange-colored paste labeled Pears and Chicken? What about an inky gel that goes by the name Blueberry Buckle? And consider, if you will, Turkey, Rice, Kale, and Mango. They take an entire three-course meal and cram it into a tiny jar. Is that even legal?

It's definitely time to make finger foods a more visible part of your baby's mealtime. They are easy to prepare, there's plenty of variety, and you don't have to worry about running out of those suspicious little jars. And not only will your newbie relish the independence of controlling his own food intake, he'll also be developing his pincer grasp, squeezing together his thumb and forefinger in order to pick things up.

Can a three-course meal be crammed into a tiny jar?

When Offering Finger Foods...

Keep the Pieces Manageable
The individual morsels need to be small enough so the baby won't choke on them. If you've been practicing baby-led weaning (see page 132), you've already introduced your little squirt to longer strips of soft foods.

Finger foods give your baby a chance to develop his pincer grasp.

Smush the Spheres

When serving round foods like chickpeas and blueberries, smush them with a spoon first. This makes them easier to chew and harder to choke on.

Have Patience

It will take time to figure out the culinary particulars of your little foodie. Let him experiment with a wide variety of flavors and textures to see which ones he gravitates toward. It may take up to ten exposures for fussy butt to decide if a particular dish gets the green light.

Put It in Piles

Scoop up the little pieces and arrange them in piles on his high-chair tray. Organizing food in individual mounds allows him to easily find his favorites and ignore the rest (which will probably end up on the floor or wall).

Give Milk After Food

At this age, a good portion of his nutrition will still come from breast milk or formula. But you'll have much more success with finger foods if you hold off on the milk until after you give him the solid stuff.

Make It Interesting

Some wee ones are slow to adapt to finger foods, and still prefer the jars. As with most baby-related activities, if you can make it seem exciting, he's more likely to take the bait. Try melting cheese on top, placing individual bites on fanned-out measuring spoons, or hiding the food under a plastic cup that the baby has to lift to access. (Pretend that lifting the cup is strictly taboo.)

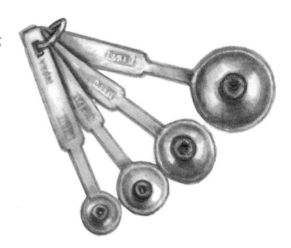

Drinking Problems

Sipping liquid from a cup is a seemingly simple task, but it demands a very precise set of movements involving hand-eye coordination, head and neck positioning, wrist and finger control, and arm flexion, not to mention lip sealing and sucking. Make one wrong move and you've got a lap full of Jamba Juice.

Many tots need a middle step to help them transition to the cup. Below are two popular options.

Straw Cups have lids with a soft silicone straw attached.

Pros: Helps them learn to drink like an adult, and the sucking develops muscles that will eventually aid them with speech.

Cons: Can take a while for the baby to figure out the straw, and they are often harder to clean than sippy cups.

Sippy Cups have lids with little plastic spouts on them. Inside the spout is a valve that controls the flow of liquid.

Pros: The spout mimics a bottle nipple, making it easier for babies to adapt. Also, they are generally more leak-proof than straw cups, so your little hellion can heave it out of his car seat with no ill effects.

Cons: Some pediatricians hesitate to recommend them because prolonged use could delay oral motor skill development as well as contribute to dental issues.

Peanut Panic

A simple mention of the word "peanut" strikes fear into the hearts of parents everywhere. You've been conditioned to worry that if your angel so much as touches a speck of nut dust, he may spontaneously combust.

Well, have no fear. Research suggests that you should have your baby try a bit of peanut butter as he is starting solid foods, because early exposure can actually PREVENT him from developing an allergy. A 2015 NIH study revealed that children who ate peanut butter throughout their childhood had an over 70% lower risk of an allergy compared to kids who avoided peanut products during that same period.

Make sure to get the go-ahead from your pediatrician beforehand. They will give you tips on how to introduce peanuts, as well as signs of potential allergic reactions.

"What did I do?"

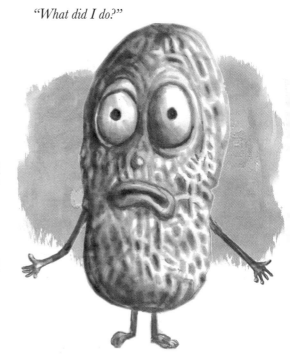

SOME GOOD OPTIONS FOR 10-TO-12-MONTH-OLDS

PROTEINS
eggs, chicken, fish, beef, pork, beans, hummus, lentils

FATS
avocado, nut butter, olive oil, egg yolks, oily fish, cheese

STARCHES
potatoes, rice, bread, pasta, plantains

FRUITS AND VEGETABLES
pretty much all of them, especially dark green and orange veggies, which provide vitamins, fiber, potassium, and many other nutrients

BABIES and
Restaurants

When dining out with your small fry, keep your expectations low. Don't expect to enjoy your meal. Don't expect to converse with your partner. Don't expect your fellow diners to be anything but irritated by your presence. And if by some miracle the baby is angelic, count your blessings and wolf down your meal as quickly as possible.

Of course, you should refrain from taking your wee one anyplace fancy. If someone is spending $50 for an entrée the size of a hockey puck, they deserve a baby-free dining experience. But if you take the urchin to a family-style restaurant and you get dirty looks from the other patrons, that's their problem, not yours.

How can you tell which restaurants are appropriate for babies and which aren't? Peruse the list of clues below.

Baby-Friendly Clues

Crayons

High chairs

Televisions

A drive-thru window

Plastic trays

Neon

"No Shirt No Shoes No Service" sign on door

Waiters with name tags

Laminated menus

Ketchup on the table

A disgruntled teen in a giant foam mouse costume

Baby-Unfriendly Clues

Tablecloths

Candles

Those giant pepper mills

Waiters who pull out your chair

Napkins made into origami swans

Water served in wineglasses

The phrase "prix fixe"

More than one fork at each place setting

A bathroom attendant

Valet parking

No guests are wearing shorts

Some genres of restaurants are known for being particularly conducive to family dining:

- **Sports bars** are good because the high noise level can mask baby shrieks, and the multiple televisions can keep him transfixed.

- **Mexican restaurants** are usually loud and casual, and some feature mariachi bands.

- **Seafood restaurants** can have fish or lobster tanks to observe, as well as those little oyster crackers that your munchkin can gnaw on.

- **Pizzerias** with open kitchens are fun because you and the baby can watch the magical pizza-making process.

- **Outdoor patios** are optimal for fussy tots, and they usually have space for all of your baby gear.

- **Hotel restaurants** provide you an easy escape into the lobby where you and the baby can blow off some steam.

- **Chinese restaurants** are almost always relaxed, and feature baby-friendly fare like fried rice. The food comes out quickly, and a fortune cookie, broken into little pieces and placed in a pile in front of the baby, can keep him busy for a good fifteen minutes.

- **Buffets** are wonderful because food can be on your chunker's plate within thirty seconds, and you can offer him a bunch of options from which to sample.

Babies love giant guitars.

How to Make It Through the Meal

Go Early Most restaurants are pretty empty from four to six, and if there are other patrons, they are usually senior citizens, who may not be able to hear a tantrum.

Pre-feed the Baby If he's starving when you enter the restaurant, you are in for a long dinner. Feed him a bit before you go out. And bring along some snacks.

Choose Your Seats Strategically Sit near an exit, so you can immediately walk out if the baby melts down. Stay away from the kitchen, so waiters aren't running by with hot trays. Booths are usually a bad idea, because his high chair will be jutting out into the aisle and blocking traffic. Putting the moppet in front of a window or fish tank may help entertain him during the meal.

Bring Activities Refuse the restaurant crayons, as they will go straight into his mouth. Instead, bring toys and books to get him through the meal. And if you happen to forget toys, remember that the resourceful dad uses whatever he has on hand.

- Sugar packets can become makeshift rattles (just don't let him try to eat them).

- A plastic to-go cup with a lid on top and an ice cube inside can fascinate him for surprisingly long periods.

- Cold spoons are effective chew toys.

- Many a desperate dad has been forced to play peek-a-boo behind a napkin.

- Saltines make impromptu pinwheels if you hold them delicately by opposite corners and blow on an edge.

Take It Outside At the first sign of tears, pick him up and head out to the parking lot until he recovers. When the next outburst hits, it's tag-team time! Suggest your partner take a shift so that both your meals can cool evenly. It's best to order items that taste good luke-warm, cold, or reheated from a to-go carton one hour later.

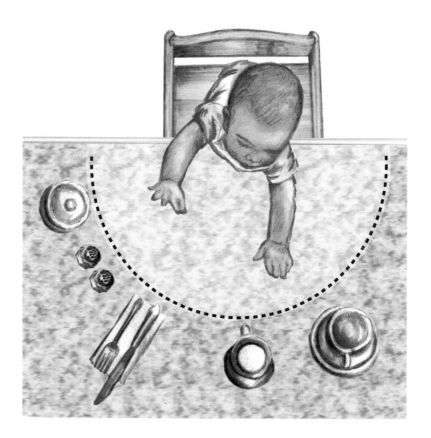

Create a No-Fly Zone No food or drinks of any kind should be allowed within the baby's lunge radius. At the beginning of the meal, place a toy near the center of the table to see how far your baby can fully extend his arm, and then make sure nothing except the baby's food and toys enter the zone. Many waiters, either absentmindedly or passive-aggressively, choose to put all the hottest items and fullest wineglasses within baby's reach, so politely ask them to adhere to the no-fly zone.

Tip Like a Boss If you've ever waited tables, then you know how disgusting it is to pick up piles of half-eaten mush from the floor. So before you leave, clean up as much as you can and compensate your server for his or her troubles in the form of a big tip. And keep in mind your baby has taken up an adult's seat, so you can tip as if he had ordered an adult-priced meal. The waiter will remember your generosity (or lack thereof) the next time you walk in.

GREAT OUTINGS
10–12 Months

Your almost-one-year-old has had his fill of sitting still and staring straight ahead. He now seeks action and adventure.

Construction Sites Dump trucks unloading, cranes hoisting girders, supports being driven into the ground, cement pouring from a mixer, and bricks being laid—you can't beat the sights, sounds, and smells of a construction site. And your baby may enjoy it, too.

Birthday Parties You'll no doubt be invited to birthday parties of similar-aged tots, and you should take every opportunity to go. It's a painless way to spend an afternoon out and about. The venue will most likely be babyproofed, they'll have snacks and fun activities, and you can compare notes with other dads. And seeing all of those remedial, average-looking babies will confirm how beautiful and talented yours is.

Water the Plants Head outside with a full watering can and pour a little bit on every plant you see on your journey. When the can is empty, fist-bump the baby on a successful mission and head back home.

Feed the Ducks Encourage your pipsqueak to throw little pieces of bread to the ducks. But keep him in your arms, because mallards can be quite aggressive, and you don't want to saddle him with a lifelong case of ornithophobia. No ducks nearby? Try the local squirrels or pigeons instead.

Big-Box Stores These stores have two things going for them: (1) they have a whole bunch of items under one roof, and (2) they are usually understaffed, leaving you free to roam and explore. The baby can start off crawling around in the carpet department, bounce on over to bedding, and try the free food samples (cut up into bite-size pieces). And when he's ready for a nap, stick him in the stroller and find an out-of-the-way display couch where you both can relax and unwind.

People-Watching You and the little one can park yourselves at a coffee shop with a steady stream of customers coming in and out. Since babies are naturally fascinated by faces, he may see it as a parade organized in his honor.

Whenever your baby does something remarkable, surprising, or funny (which will be happening more and more at this age), immediately record a voice memo. You'll want to remember these priceless moments, because you s¹ ... never pass this way again, at least with this child.

SKILL Builders
10–12
Months

The Dad Hammock

Lay a blanket, towel, or sheet on the floor and place the bambino in the center. Grab the two corners nearest his head with one hand and the two corners nearest his feet with the other. Make sure you've got a tight grip, and that he can peek out through a crack in the center. Lift the blanket and gently swing him back and forth, being careful to avoid furniture.

If your baby is at all hesitant or skeptical about this activity, first demo it with his stuffed animals, and then ask if he wants a turn.

Builds trust, spatial awareness, and Dad's traps and delts.

Document Shredding

Have a stack of old bills, statements, receipts, credit card applications, and other personal paperwork that needs to be destroyed? Turn it into a shredding party! Rip up a few documents to show him how it's done. (Many babies find this hilarious.) Then, half-tear some pages and let him finish the job. Not today, identity thieves!

Builds fine motor skills, mimicry, relieves stress.

The Sticker Monster

Procure a few packs of reusable baby-friendly stickers or a pad of sticky notes. Help your little vandal peel off the stickers, and then let him cover you head to toe, transforming you into an avant-garde art piece. And when the project is complete, take a selfie with the artist, and place the stickers back on the sheet so Mom can have a turn.

After a round of sticker monster, many a dad has unknowingly left the house with a cartoon animal stuck behind his ear.

Builds hand-eye coordination and fine motor skills.

The Decoy Drawer

What objects are the most vital to your day-to-day existence? If you are like most dads, it's probably your phone, wallet, keys, credit cards, and perhaps the TV remote or game controller. Somehow your tiny troublemaker senses the power these objects possess and will take every opportunity to seize and/or destroy them.

You decide to buy the baby colorful plastic versions of his own. That way he'll have his toys to play with, and you'll have yours. But of course he immediately throws aside the impostors and makes a beeline back to the genuine articles.

That's why you need to create a decoy drawer full of old phones, remotes, wallets, keys, credit cards, and other coveted gadgets. The drawer should be at a good baby height, and all items need to be real but nonfunctioning. That way when he opens the drawer, he'll think he's hit the mother lode.

You've got to sell the fake.

But this deception won't work unless you sell the fake. Every time he goes into the drawer, give him a look of reproach that reassures him that he's doing something strictly off-limits.

You can create a decoy drawer in almost any room in the house. It will provide hours of fun for the baby and give you some much-needed downtime.

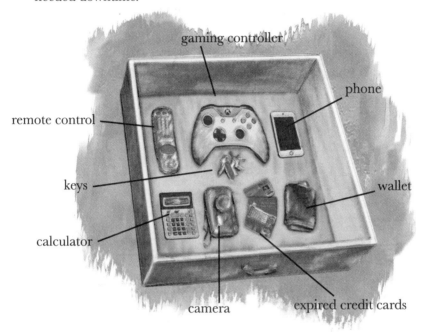

Make sure all items in your decoy drawer are free of small parts that could break off and become a choking hazard. Remove batteries and crazy-glue all battery covers.

Decoy Drawers for Every Room

Kitchen Plastic cups and saucers, spatulas, soup containers, wooden spoons, egg cartons.

Bathroom Old washed-out shampoo bottles, toothbrushes, combs and soft brushes, a plastic soap dish, washcloths, a childproof hand-held mirror.

Home Office Unlock one drawer of the file cabinet and fill the folders with scrap paper, flyers, receipts, and junk mail. (Install rubber stoppers to prevent finger slams and make sure baby Einstein doesn't eat the paper.)

RIGGING EMERGENCY
DIAPERS

It's four a.m. and Whine-a-saurus rex is blubbering. You guess it's a discomfort cry, and your theory is confirmed by the pungent smell that hits you when you enter the room. You reach into the drawer for a clean diaper and come up with—nothing. You are completely out, and you are going to have to wait until morning to restock.

You assume this won't happen to you? You'll be lucky if it happens only once.

The prepared dad knows how to rig up a makeshift diaper for just such an emergency. Your homemade nappy won't need to be super absorbent, ultra comfortable, or aesthetically pleasing. It just needs to work well enough to get you through the night, so you can mobilize at dawn to buy the real deal.

Instructions

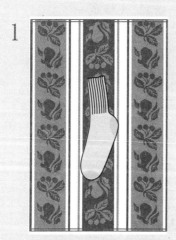
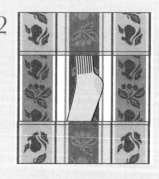

1. Lay out the dish towel and place the sock in the center, lengthwise.

2. Fold over the sides of the dish towel to make a square.

3. Lay baby on top of the dish towel, then fold the bottom part up between his legs so it rests on top of his midsection.

4. Tuck the front corners inside of the back corners and secure with

What you are going to need:

1 clean dish towel

1 clean cotton sweat sock

1 roll of duct tape

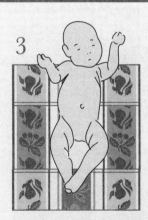

3

4

You'll need to have a pair of safety scissors on hand. Otherwise, it may be difficult to extricate the baby.

duct tape. Make sure that it's not too tight, and that the duct tape doesn't get near the baby's skin.

5. If the diaper is too saggy in the crotch area, use extra duct tape to close the space.

6. If you want to make the diaper water-resistant (which is highly advisable), simply duct-tape as much of the surface area as you can, making sure that baby's skin won't be chafed.

ADVANCED
Changing Maneuvers

With older babies you often have to modify your diaper-changing techniques.

The Standing Diaper Change

Obsessed with mobility, chunkers this age don't appreciate being forced to lie down for a diaper change. So they'll writhe around, looking for any way possible to get free of your grip, even if it means taking a header off the changing table. In these situations, the prepared dad makes use of the standing diaper change, which is meant for a urine-filled diaper but can work for most poop diapers as well, as long as you're careful.

Procedure

1. Pile a bunch of toys on a couch or a heavy chair.

2. Start loudly playing with the toys, luring Mr. Inquisitive over to the staging area. If you forcibly drag him over, you'll tip your hand, and he'll know something's up.

3. Lean him up against the chair. Always keep one hand on him in case he starts to tilt. Then quickly unsnap or unzip his pant legs and tuck them into the neck of his shirt to give you clear access to the diaper.

4. Change and wipe as quickly as humanly possible, before he gets bored and tries to bolt. And more importantly, you have no idea if he's got any ammo left, so you want to severely limit the time he is bottomless.

The Standing Lap Change

The standing lap change is for those times when you can't administer the standing diaper change. You might employ it while sitting in a crowded train, on a hike, or in a sports arena.

For this maneuver, you remain seated while the baby stands in your lap. He's facing you, leaning on your shoulders or chest for support. The procedure is similar to the standing diaper change, but since the baby is looking directly at you, you must find a different way to keep him occupied and cooperative during the change.

One way to distract the baby: become a mobile

If you're wearing a baseball cap, turn yourself into a human mobile by clipping a pacifier cord to the brim and dangling a toy from the cord.

Big League Blowouts

Every once in a while your baby will stun you with a volcanic liquid poop that will quickly overflow the diaper and shoot up his back. This event is known as a big league blowout.

If he blows out at home, pray that he's not inhabiting your couch at the time. And if he blows out on the road, pray that you've brought enough wipes to contain the mess. More than one dad has had to sacrifice his socks for the cause.

An immediate bath is the best solution. Barring that, lay the kiddo on a changing pad or brown towel and quickly remove his soiled clothing. And for obvious reasons, always take a onesie off from the bottom, never over the head. Use the unsoiled areas of the clothing to mop up the mess. Throw the clothes in a plastic bag (you should have at least two or three with you at all times), and start cleaning with wipes or a wet washcloth if you have access to one. Do a basic sweep first, and then move on to detailed work once the muck is under control.

Changing Stations

You are probably very familiar with this symbol, having seen it in many public spaces, including restaurants, office buildings, stores, and malls. For new moms, it's a glorious vision. There is a changing table in the ladies' room.

Yet this image—the men's room changing station symbol—is a much less common occurrence. The question is—why?

Because our research provided no definitive answers on the topic, we are forced to surmise that it was a decision based on the antiquated notion that women are considered the caretakers, and by extension, the diaper changers.

But the tide is slowly turning. More and more states are passing laws that require changing tables in both men's and women's restrooms (although many of these laws apply only to new or renovated buildings). Designated family restrooms are becoming more common. And nationally, Congress passed the Bathrooms Accessible In Every Situation Act (it's called the BABIES Act, although we're still searching for the second B). This law mandates that every bathroom in a federal building has a changing station.

In the meantime, you'll need to find a spot to change in the wild, because you sure as hell aren't going to use the floor of a public men's room. And although we'd never dare suggest a desperate dad go into an empty ladies' room for a quick nappy swap, it's been known to happen.

Making Your Baby LAUGH

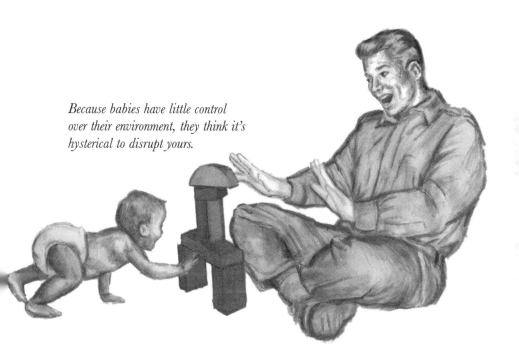

Because babies have little control over their environment, they think it's hysterical to disrupt yours.

Just as your partner is uniquely qualified to breastfeed, you are uniquely qualified to provide comic relief for your sprite. That's not saying your partner won't be able to conjure up some baby belly laughs. But when it comes to understanding the infant sense of humor, you've got the edge, because it's probably not that different from your own. If you've ever enjoyed *Looney Tunes* cartoons, piñata fail videos, or any Adam Sandler movie, then you've got all the tools you need to create your own baby stand-up routine.

You'll discover his favorite jokes through trial and error, and sometimes completely by accident. A random sneeze may trigger hysterics, and an apple rolling off a table may send him over the edge. But if you're ever stuck for material, here are some time-honored gags, broken down into categories, that will hopefully leave your baby drooling for more.

Dad as Baby

- Put his pacifier in your mouth backwards, try to suck on it, and then spit it out in frustration.

- While he's drinking his bottle, try to drink from the other end.

- Crawl around on the floor and have your partner chase you.

Dad as Complete Moron

- Try to put the baby's pants on your head, or the baby's shoes on the dog.

- Put a toy on your head and pretend to look for it. When it falls to the floor, act startled.

- Show him pictures of various animals but get their sounds wrong. "The cow says oink!" (Eventually he'll catch on.)

Dad as Animal

- Growl like a dog and pull off baby's sock using only your teeth. Have him try to get the sock out of your mouth.

- Turn your finger into a buzzing bee and have it land first on your nose and then on baby's. Keep shooing it off.

- Make believe one of your hands is a lobster claw and have it snap at the baby and then yourself. Make it latch on to your nose and not let go.

The Revenge of Dad

- Pretend to eat the baby like a giant ear of corn.

- Smell his feet, make a nauseated face, and push them away, saying, "DIS-gusting!"

- Curl the baby like a barbell, and when he gets close to your mouth, blow a giant raspberry on his stomach.

Baby Causing Pain to Dad

- Build a block tower, and when he knocks it over, burst into tears.

- Lying next to the baby, close your eyes and snore loudly. When he pokes you, lift your head up and say, "I'm trying to get some sleep around here!" and lie back down. Repeat.

- Hold a piece of the baby's food close to him, and pretend not to notice when he takes it from your hand. Then look at your empty hand and say, "Hey, that's my food!"

Dad Causing Pain to Dad

- Hit yourself in the head with an empty plastic bottle, and then imitate Homer Simpson's "D'oh!"

- Trip over one of the baby's toys and do a big pratfall onto the couch.

- Hold a water pistol or spray bottle in your hand. Point it at your face, look at the trigger, and say, "I wonder what this does." Squirt yourself and scream.

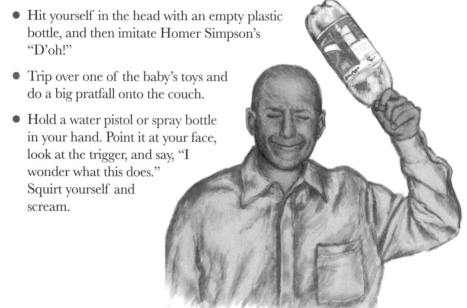

A joke occurs when you expect one thing and you get something completely different. Most babies under seven or eight months old don't understand jokes, because they have no expectations. They accept everything at face value. In short, they're gullible. This is why there are so few successful baby comedy clubs.

Whippersnapper

Some babies are born skeptics. They will not give up a laugh, even after ten minutes of your best material. That's when you've got to break out the big guns and literally whip him into a frenzy.

The following routine is best performed on a towel or shower curtain on the floor, unless you want pasteurized dairy product mushed into your carpet.

Simply grab a can of whipped cream, and spray a dollop onto his hand. The sudden whoosh sound combined with the instant fluffy white cloud should short-circuit his brain and start him giggling. And when he puts his hand to his mouth to taste that sweetness, it could very well cause a laughing fit. Subsequently spray dollops onto his elbows, knees, feet, and belly. Just think of him as a giant strawberry shortcake.

And when you're done, its bath time!

FLYIN' and Cryin'

Let those around you share the responsibility of entertaining the baby.

Tired of spending all of your time cooped up in the house with your offspring? Instead, why not spend some time cooped up with him in a flying metal tube? If nothing else, do it for the sheer pleasure of watching your fellow passengers' terrified reactions as you board, baby in hand, and walk down the aisle toward them. For added effect, make direct eye contact with every single person.

When traveling by plane, the most that any parent can hope for is a quiet kiddie. Employ the tactics on the following pages to keep him happy and serene.

Choose Your Seats Wisely

When booking a flight, keep in mind the following:

- Although your baby is not required to sit in his own seat until two years of age, the FAA recommends purchasing one and securing his car seat to it, which is safer in case of extreme turbulence. But since that is such a rare occurrence, many dads choose the frugal route and keep the baby on their lap. If you don't buy a seat for your baby, you and your partner could try the old travel hack of reserving the window and aisle seats in the same row, leaving the middle seat open. Middles always fill up last, and even if someone has reserved it, as soon as they see the baby, they'll beg the flight attendant for reassignment.

- The bulkhead row offers the most legroom, and having a wall in front of you is a blessing, especially when el diablo decides to throw his toys around. If you put in a request, some airlines will provide bassinets (a.k.a. sky cots) that attach directly to the bulkhead.

- If you sit near the restrooms, it tends to be loud, but there's usually some extra space to move around. And since babies love people-watching, the near-constant traffic may keep him entertained. You can play peek-a-boo with passengers as they open and close the bathroom door (whether they like it or not). The restroom mirror can also be a fun diversion. But whatever you do, do not flush the toilet. There is no scarier sound to a tot.

- Parents with babies are not allowed to sit in the exit rows. Presumably this is because after an hour with a screaming infant, those seated next to you might try to pull the emergency latch and jump out.

Even if he will be sitting on your lap, you'll need to get the squirt a boarding pass from a kiosk or ticket counter.

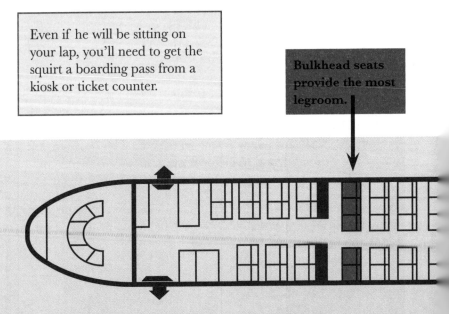

Bulkhead seats provide the most legroom.

Increase the Odds of Sleep

- Time your trip with his nap or suck it up and take the red-eye.

- Get to the airport early, and run him ragged. This won't be hard to do, as babies are energized by the wide-open spaces, moving walkways, and carpeted hallways of airports.

- Board last, even though you are allowed to board first. Either you or your partner get on with all of the gear while the other one wears him out in the waiting area.

- The sound of the plane is a natural source of white noise and may induce drowsiness.

- You can try dosing your baby into dreamland with baby Benadryl or Tylenol, but the drug can also have the opposite effect, acting like baby Red Bull. And that's the last thing you need on a long flight. (Always consult your doctor before administering any medicine.)

Feed During Takeoffs and Landings

In order to balance the pressure in his ears, he should be on the breast or bottle during takeoffs and especially landings. If he's not hungry, a pacifier can also work to relieve the pressure. And if he refuses to suck, he'll feel pain in his ears and start crying, an activity that will also help to balance the pressure.

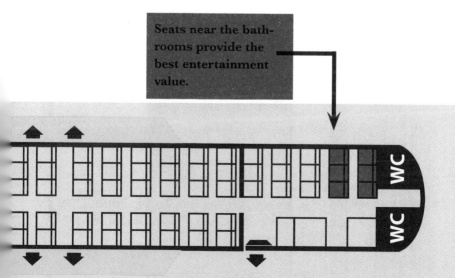

Seats near the bathrooms provide the best entertainment value.

If you were airport security and you saw this bag, what would you think?

You are allowed to bring full baby bottles through security. And if you need to heat up a bottle on the plane, you can ask the flight attendant to warm it in a cup of hot water.

You might also want to take powdered formula onto the plane. Some dads pre-measure the powder into little plastic bags, but this might not be the best idea if you want to clear airport security in a timely manner.

Prepare for Flying Fluids

Because the risk of airsickness is always high, remember to pack three or four extra outfits for him. And take an extra shirt for yourself in case you happen to get vomited upon. Also bring plastic bags, wipes, and paper towels for containment purposes.

Most planes have changing tables in the bathrooms. If yours does not, try changing him on a pad or towel over the closed toilet lid. If that's too cramped, you may need to stage it right on your seat while standing over him.

When exiting the plane, grab a few airsickness bags. They are great for storing wet or dirty clothes, rancid diapers, and other baby-related debris.

Deploy Distractions at Regular Intervals

Go to a discount store and buy a bunch of rubber and plastic baby-safe toys. Wrap them up in paper bags. As soon as you notice puddin' pop getting fussy, hand him a new toy to unwrap. He will get very excited by the gifts. Figure on one toy for each half hour of flight time.

Some other dad-tested distractions:

- Buy some press-on window decals for the baby to stick to the window and peel off.

- Deflated blow-up toys take up almost no space.

- Bring a small plastic tackle box with individual compartments, and put one Cheerio in each for the munchkin to retrieve and consume.

- A device loaded with baby-friendly videos is also recommended. Even if you don't normally allow screen time, now would be the perfect exception to the rule.

- Put a blanket on the floor and let him wriggle around down there for a while.

- For your fellow passengers' sake, don't bring anything that squeaks, sings, talks, or makes loud animal sounds.

- If you run out of distractions, try making a puppet out of an airsickness bag.

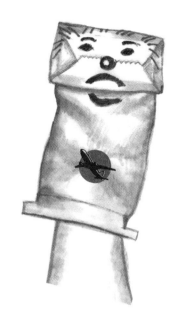

Force Others to Entertain the Baby

Hold him up directly in front of the passengers nearest you and see if anyone bites. If you keep him there for an uncomfortably long time, someone is bound to look up from their tablet and force a smile. That's when you say to the baby, "I think somebody wants to play peek-a-boo." Look at it this way: If everyone wants a quiet baby, they're going to have to suck it up and pull their weight. It takes a village.

Bring Baby-Holding Devices

Airlines let you bring your stroller or car seat right up to the plane and check it at the gate. Having a stroller with you at all times is important, particularly when you are stuck in an airport because your connecting flight is three hours late, or you're held up waiting for dogs to come and sniff your powdered formula.

Some new parents bring gift bags for everyone seated around them, pre-apologizing for the baby. We don't recommend this approach, as it reinforces the idea that babies don't belong on airplanes. Now if you are flying with a conspiracy theorist who may freak out and need to be duct-taped to the seat, goody bags full of alcohol are definitely in order.

Hotel, Motel, HOLIDAY INN

It's worth staying at a hotel with your baby for the long hallways alone. Hotel hallways are to ten- to twelve-month-olds what empty swimming pools are to skateboarders: ideal places to hone their skills. The walls are smooth and even and the floors are thickly carpeted, cushioning the inevitable face-plant. And every journey can end in a visit to the ice machine—an all-time baby favorite combining equal parts sight, sound, touch, and taste. (You Airbnb parents don't know what you're missing.)

Hotels can provide a much-needed break for dads, too. It's refreshing to see your progeny trashing someone else's place for once. But before turning him loose in his new habitat, there are two major issues that you'll need to address: sleep and safety.

Hotel Sleep Solutions

• **Bring a portable crib** While many hotels provide cribs, they can be old and rickety, and the mattresses may have seen one too many accidents. For peace of mind, bring along a travel crib, and have him take a few naps in it beforehand to get him acclimated.

• **Make the room conducive to sleep** To keep the room dark, take some hangers from the closet and use them to clamp the curtains together. Bring a white noise machine and night light if you use them at home. And in case the curtains aren't dark enough, bring some large black trash bags and tape them over the windows. Will housekeeping think you are a family of serial killers? Probably.

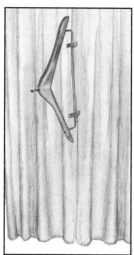

• **Spring for a suite** If your budget allows, procure a suite so that you and the baby don't have to sleep in the same room. That way, once he's down, you won't have to tiptoe around in the dark for three hours like a cat burglar.

• **Stow the baby** If you can't get a suite, put as much distance between yourself and the baby as possible. Perhaps the closet is big enough to fit a portable crib. Some folks stick the baby in the bathroom, which is a great idea until you need to go. And most hotels frown on you peeing off the balcony.

Hotel hangers are not just for clothes.

• **Bring bathroom activities** This is for you, not the baby. If you all end up in one room, you and your partner may be hanging out in the bathroom for a few hours once he's down. In lieu of deep talks about your future, you might want to bring a game of Scrabble, a chessboard, or a deck of cards. Loser has to cover the next middle-of-the-night wake-up.

• **Take shifts** Just because one of you is stuck in the room doesn't mean you both have to suffer. While your partner goes down to the hotel bar to fend off conventioneers, you can hang out in the room, listen to podcasts, read the Bible, or watch a show with earbuds. After an hour or so, switch.

The Four-Minute Babyproof

Babyproofing your hotel room won't take nearly as long as babyproofing your home (or an Airbnb for that matter). Because you'll only be there for a short period of time, your installations should be fairly easy to remove. Some hotels supply childproofing kits, but most expect you to do it yourself, a task that should take you less than five minutes. The most important item you'll need is painter's tape (don't use duct tape unless you want to get a bill for room damages).

Your baby may assume the minibar is for mini-people.

- Before you let the baby crawl around the room, sweep the floor for hazardous items like paper clips and loose change. Place the coffee-maker, hair dryer, and iron out of reach.

- Use painter's tape to cover up outlets, tape drawers and cabinets shut, and secure the minibar. To protect your little guy's head from sharp edges, bring along extra baby socks, fold them in half, and tape them over all furniture corners that are at the baby's height or below.

- Tape a big X across the sliding glass doors leading to the balcony to let your daredevil know that he can't head straight out. And make sure balcony doors are locked. Wrangle and tape up all drape, blind, phone, and lamp cords. Secure closet doors by wrapping a pipe cleaner around both knobs and twisting.

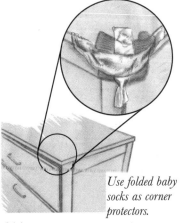

Use folded baby socks as corner protectors.

- We suggest keeping the bathroom door closed and off-limits. If little Houdini has figured out how to open doors, put one of your socks over the bathroom doorknob. He will have a tough time getting enough traction to twist it open.

Remember to tip housekeeping well. Babies can do more damage to hotel rooms than metal bands, and you should compensate accordingly.

How to Neutralize a RUNNING BABY

Some one-year-olds walk, and others sprint. Undaunted by crowded aisles, steep escalators, and busy intersections, they forge ahead, like Shackleton, toward the great unknown.

As a father, you admire your baby's tenacity. But as a parent who wants to bring home a live child, you must somehow restrain him. Baby leashes exist, but you might want to save that option as a last resort.

The best way to deal with an AWOL threat is to outfit him in clothes that you can get a grip on, such as:

- Hooded sweatshirts
- Overalls
- Suspenders
- Pants with belt loops

When a potentially hazardous situation arises, just grab hold and he's immobile. (When holding the hood, only use gentle tugs.) Then, when the danger passes, let go, and he's once again free to taste-test every surface in the mall.

Use your baby's hood as a makeshift leash.

Camping with Your CUB

Don't let your baby be an excuse to retire your tent and sleeping bag. On the contrary, camping with your cub can be a great experience for the whole family. You'll get the thrill of introducing him to the wonders of nature, and he'll have the opportunity to eat a much better variety of dirt than he gets at home.

You're going to be hauling plenty of gear, especially if you decide to go backpacking in the woods. One of you will have to carry the baby, and the other will have to lug everything else. Trudging through the forest with the baby in one backpack and the oversized load of equipment in the other, you may feel like mountain guides your baby has hired for an expedition.

Setting Up Camp

- Pick a campsite that's a good distance away from other campers. You don't want your baby's three a.m. screams waking up your fellow campmates. Conversely, you don't want your fellow campmates' three a.m. screams waking up your baby.

- You'll need a secure place to put him while setting up camp. If you pitch your tent first, it can function as an instant playpen. But the baby may be happier in a portable crib. He'll be able to pull himself up and peruse the great outdoors.

- Once you're set up, put some long pants on the imp and let him crawl around the environs with you in tow. Just make sure he doesn't try to eat any plants, stick his hand down any snake holes, befriend any fire ants . . . or firepits. But allow him to get filthy. A layer of dirt will do him some good.

- You can use baby-safe bug repellent on kids over two months old, and baby sunscreen at six months. (Apply sunscreen before repellent.) And because you may encounter ticks, mosquitoes, and poison ivy, oak, and sumac—not to mention the blazing sun— you should bedeck your little scout in long clothing and a wide-brimmed hat for optimal protection.

Sleeping Outdoors

- Keep in mind that a two-person tent will be very uncomfortable for two adults and a portable crib. Get a four- or six-person model.

- Be prepared to get a terrible night's sleep, at least for the first few excursions. And if things go better than expected, count your blessings.

- Keep a flashlight next to you in your sleeping bag, so you can turn it on as soon as he starts to cry. Babies aren't used to the pitch blackness and the spooky sounds of the woods at night, so they can get easily rattled.

Take an inflatable baby pool along with you. It has a multitude of uses and deflates to almost nothing. It can serve as a:

- Bathtub (he's gonna get some dirt on him)
- Swimming pool
- Play area
- Diaper changing station
- Impromptu sandbox

Always supervise the baby when he's in the pool, no matter what he's doing.

- If you've got a yard, help him get acclimated to outdoor sleeping by staging a dry run with the portable crib in the tent.

- Dress the baby in a sleep sack or a wearable sleeping bag if the nights get cold.

Waste Disposal

Most state parks have a carry-in/carry-out policy, which means you can't leave any trash behind. You'll be putting most of it in plastic bags and hauling it around with you, but what do you do with poop-filled diapers?

The best solution is to bury the poop and then place the diaper in several layers of bags. When burying poop, dig a hole around six inches deep and at least 100 feet from a water source.

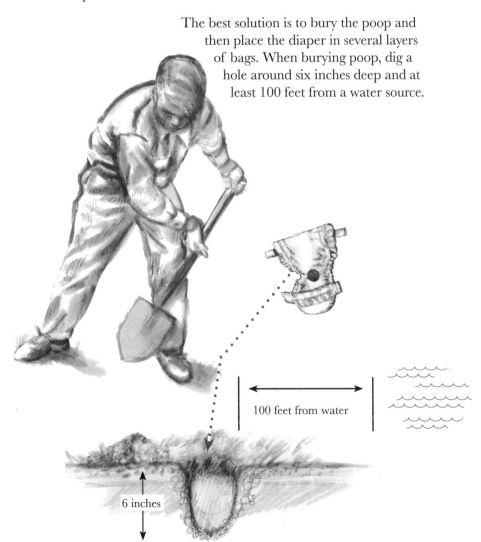

100 feet from water

6 inches

The Baby Backpack

Before buying a backpack, bring your baby to the store and go on a mini-hike through the aisles with him securely in the pack. If it's not comfortable after five minutes, it certainly won't be comfortable on a three-hour trek through the woods. (Babies need to weigh around sixteen pounds and be able to sit up on their own before they can be carried in a backpack.)

Some things to look for in a baby pack:

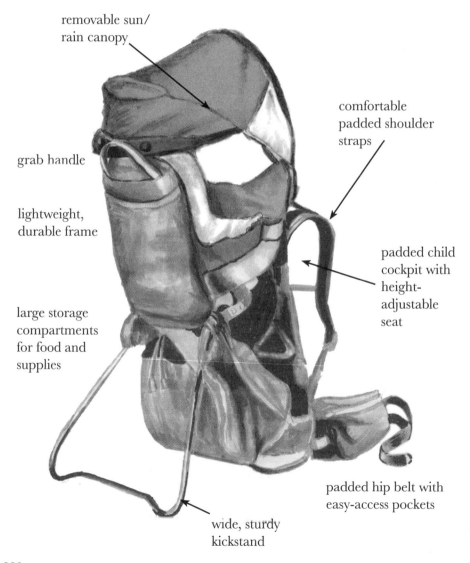

removable sun/ rain canopy

comfortable padded shoulder straps

grab handle

lightweight, durable frame

padded child cockpit with height-adjustable seat

large storage compartments for food and supplies

padded hip belt with easy-access pockets

wide, sturdy kickstand

Seven Things to Consider Before Embarking on a Hike

1. Never hike alone with your baby. If you happen to twist your ankle, you want another adult to be there.

2. The total weight of the backpack, baby included, should be less than forty-eight pounds. Note that baby weight is different from gear weight. If you are not careful, the baby's constant shifting can throw you off-balance. Test it on a stroll around the neighborhood before trail hiking.

3. Dress your pollywog more warmly than yourself. Remember that you are moving around, while he is basically luggage.

4. The backpack provides your baby a perfect angle to spit up right into your shirt and down your back. It's best not to go hiking right after he's had a big meal, because the jiggling can bring everything up . . . and then down.

5. If it's hot out, use the canopy, and make sure to keep him hydrated. To cool him off, fill up a spray bottle with lukewarm water so you can reach back and mist him once in a while.

6. If you are going to be out for longer than an hour, pack a blanket. Take the baby out so he can stretch his legs and crawl around.

7. Stay on the beaten path, and always stick closely to marked trails, no matter how confident you are in your hiking abilities. Having a little monster on your back is extreme enough.

Bears and Babies

Bears and babies do not mix well, so it would be best to avoid encountering a bear if you can help it. But if you are camping anywhere near bear country, follow these simple guidelines to prevent a confrontation:

Avoid Startling a Bear Most bears will only attack if startled. When walking through the woods, sing loud songs with the baby so that the bears will hear you coming. Clip a baby rattle or clangy toy to your belt to add to the noise level.

Keep Food and Garbage out of Reach Stow all food, milk, and formula in the trunk of your car or hang it from a tree branch at least ten feet from the ground and four feet out from the tree trunk. Do the same with soiled diapers and other strong-smelling garbage as well. (You can also buy a bear-proof container if you don't mind lugging it around.)

Keep Away from Dead Things When exploring with the nipper, never approach a dead animal. It could be a fresh bear kill, and the perp might be lurking close by.

If You See a Bear, Make Your Presence Known Remain still, and talk calmly. Slowly wave your arms over your head. You want the bear to register you as a human and not a prey animal. No shrieks or sudden movements. Don't try to run or climb a tree. Bears are better than you at both.

Make Yourself Look as Large as Possible With the baby on your back, the bear may think you're a two-headed monster.

If the Bear Is Stationary, Retreat Sideways Slowly shuffle away sideways, which is less threatening to a bear, and will allow you to look at him and the path behind you at the same time. If the bear follows, stop and hold your ground.

Carry Bear Spray As an insurance policy, clamp a can of bear spray to your backpack belt so you can get to it quickly.

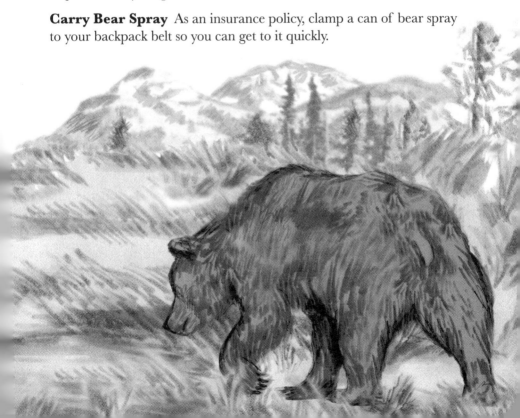

The First
BIRTHDAY
PARTY

As the saying goes, "All first birthday parties are surprise parties." The baby of honor will have no clue what the heck is going on, and a few weeks from now will completely forget it ever happened.

But don't let that stop you from celebrating, because you and your partner deserve it. You made it through the first year, which is a remarkable feat. So have some friends and family over to mark this milestone. And even though the baby won't appreciate the effort, the adorable pictures of him wearing a stupid hat with frosting all over his face will last a lifetime.

A few tips on throwing a successful first birthday party:

SIZE Keep it manageable, especially when it comes to other babies. The general rule of thumb is that the number of baby guests at the party should equal the child's age plus one. So invite two babies who have fun parents.

TIMING Don't schedule the party during his normal nap time, thinking that the adrenaline will charge him up. He'll either have a meltdown or sleep through the whole thing. And don't schedule it for too late in the day. After eating a few fistfuls of frosting, he'll need some time to detox before bedtime.

GIFTS If your home is already full of baby stuff, tell your guests not to bring gifts. Instead, gift wrap things you have laying around the house—a banana, a spatula, a random toy they forgot about last month, or a hard-boiled egg. You'd be surprised how excited babies get opening anything!

ENTERTAINMENT One-year-olds don't need costumed characters. When your baby sees Elmo on a screen, he's only six inches tall. And when a six-foot-tall Elmo walks into the room, it may trigger a full-scale panic attack. Hiring a magician is a waste, because to babies, everything is magic. Mini ball pits are fine until one kid pukes, and then it becomes a mini hazmat area.

So what activity DO we recommend? Get a mini mirror ball and a bubble machine, and when the time feels right, dim the lights, crank up some of your favorite tunes, and throw a baby rave. You'll be glad you did.

FOOD Smash cakes are miniature birthday cakes made specifically for a baby to shove his hands into and get all messy. They make for classic first birthday photos. Provide snacks for the babies and adults, and have wine and beer options on hand. And before the party ends, get everyone to raise their glasses, clink them against your baby's bottle, and drink a toast to toddlerhood.

The New Year's PANDA

CONGRATULATIONS!

You've reached the end of your baby's first year (at least in book form). Your accomplishment deserves a reward. In lieu of cash, you are going to receive a powerful fatherhood secret, until now known only to a handful of the most resourceful dads out there. This secret will not only save you thousands of dollars over your lifetime, but it will also become a highly anticipated family tradition that can be passed down from generation to generation. And it's called the New Year's Panda.

The New Year's Panda was created by an ingenious dad who thought it unfair that everything went on sale right after Christmas, the day after he needed it. So he started looking for a way to take advantage of the steep post-holiday markdowns and keep his kids happy at the same time. Thus the New Year's Panda was born.

In early December of the following year, he sat his children down and told them that on New Year's Eve, a large fuzzy panda visits the homes of children who didn't get everything they wanted for the holidays and fills in their wish lists. And to make sure the panda doesn't skip over your house, you need to put some licorice sticks on the front doorstep to make him feel welcome.

Now, your baby may be too young to fully comprehend the glory of the New Year's Panda, but it's never too early to start the tradition. If you begin now, by the time he's ready for kindergarten, it will be an essential part of your family's holiday ritual.

CONCLUSION

The past year seems like a blur, doesn't it? It's almost impossible to remember the days when your big bambino was a newborn and could fit in the crook of your arm. Just a year ago, you were holding a squirming bundle of flesh, and now you're holding a real live person who can actually communicate and get around independently and perform amusing antics.

Not only has the tadpole grown this past year, but you've grown as well. Do you remember the sheer terror you were feeling those first days home from the hospital? Well, look at you now. You're a seasoned veteran. And we hope you pass along your newfound wisdom to others. When you see a clueless rookie dad in distress, don't snicker at him from afar. Do what you can to lend a hand or offer a word of sage advice. And maybe even recommend a particular book specifically designed to help new dads just like him? Or even better—be a big shot and order him a copy of his own!

We congratulate you on a job well done, and sincerely hope that this was the best year of your life (we already know it was the best year of your baby's life). After what you've been through, you deserve some well-earned leave time. But unfortunately, you won't be getting any. Because fatherhood is a 24-7-365 endeavor, and you signed on for the long haul. So hoist up your potty seat and be prepared for year two!

ACKNOWLEDGMENTS

We'd like to thank Robert Messenger, Eamon Dolan, Tzipora Chein, Douglas Johnson, Paul Dippolito, and all the talented, supportive folks at Simon & Schuster. Grateful acknowledgments go out to our agent and friend of almost thirty years Todd Shuster, as well as the always-insightful Jack Haug, and everyone at Aevitas Creative Management. And special thanks to our original editor, Rob Weisbach, who, over twenty years ago, championed the book and helped bring it to life.

Our deepest appreciation goes out to content reviewer Dr. Rebekah Diamond. Dr. Diamond took time out from her busy life as a hospital pediatrician, assistant professor at Columbia University, and mom, to pore through our book and make sure all the info is up to date and baby-safe.

Thanks to the *Be Prepared* Twentieth Anniversary research and development team, consisting of Bryan Paulk, Jamie Agin, Alison Flierl, and Marcy Greenberg. We greatly appreciate your analysis, insights, and humor.

We'd also like to thank Jimmy Kimmel, Meg Donaldson, Jeremy Kareken, Mike Royce, Jon Bines, Kevin Johnson, Herb Emanuelson, Jeff Boyd, Jonathan Stirling, Matt Ahern, John Lewis, Dave Brause, Jon Mysel, Mike Astrachan, Neal Lieberman, Lenny Levy, John Mertens, Paul Flynn, Dave Goldman, Steve Heller, Pablo Martinez, Bob Goetz, Sam Joseph, Andrew Kennedy, Don Hamrahi, Wayne Catan, Howie Allen, Leland Brandt, Joe Badalamente, Jeff Felmus, Faye Hess, Todd Hansen, Mike Litsky, Dan Varrichione, Sean Martin Hingston, Molly McNearney, Danny Ricker, Josh Halloway, Rick Winters, David Caminear, Johnny Lampert, John Diresta, Dave Hirsch, Madison Rogers, Tim Mangan, Andrew Tsiouris, Roland Paradis, Mike Rozen, Garrison Schwartz, Ken Friedson, Charles Bonerbo, Annabelle Boyd, Jacob Boyd, Leigh Hayden, Pete Tuneski, Prescott Tuneski, Tess Tuneski,

Jeffrey Shaw, Roy and Beth Markham and their New Year's Panda, Eva Hulme, Holley and Russ Flagg, Lenny and Barbara Grodin, Lucinda Knox, Jodi Lamourine-Fleisher, Elliot and Judy Brause, Lisa Brause, William Stephenson, Ellie and Don Jacobs, Evie Barkin, Joe Clancy, Evan Shweky, Steve Gibbs, Steve Brykman, Raegan McCain, Jon Jacobs, Ellen Lenson, Oona Stern, Monique and Sergio Savarese, Joan Schultz, Adele Phillips, Brian Stern, Chris Mazzilli, Peter Shapiro, Amelia Webster, Derek Lugo, Jude Gallagher, Frank Bozzo, Susan and John Javens, Carol Danilowicz, Petra Dielewicz, Rob Carson, Beth and Johnny Garcia and the Manhattan Kids Club, Ilana Ruskay-Kidd and the Manhattan JCC, Suzanne Reiss, Daryle Connors, Stacey Fredericks, Kiki Schaeffer, Matt Strauss, the Sol Goldman YMCA, Schneider's Baby Store, Felina Rakowski-Gallagher and the Upper Breast Side, Mike Abt and Abt Electronics, Derrick Neville and Circuit City, Manny Pagan, Ben Kim, Alexandra Jacobs, Jessica Nooney, Corlette James and everyone at the Small World Preschool, John Rodadero, John and Patty Wrajec, Lillie Rosenthal, the Blodgett family, the Dexter family, the Lamourine family, Dawn Hutchins, Jean DeMerit, Carla Alcabes, Michelle Larrier, Jordan Rubin, Eva Dorsey and Jane's Exchange, Catherine Cetrangolo, Jeffrey Benoit, Alec Lawson, Suzanne Ball, Yvonne Suzuki Licopoli, Jim Mangan, Sarah Pillow, Gail San Juan, Lisa Cerone, Ann Clark Espuelas, JoAnn Egan Neil, Anna Vocino, Sarah Benesch, Michele Lussier, Nancy Coffey, Lois Keller, Nancy Haber Nickerson, Liz Abbe and Lew Schneider, Julia Diller, Marlene McGuirt, Rachelle Carson-Begley, Alicen Sullivan, and Peg McCormick.

And most important, we'd like to thank our daughter Maddie, who was a great sport during the nine months we neglected her so we could write a parenting book. Over twenty years have passed, and we are so proud of the fabulous person you've become.

INDEX

ABOUT THE AUTHORS

Gary Greenberg is a writer and supervising producer at *Jimmy Kimmel Live!*, where he's worked for over twenty years. He's the author of the national bestseller *The Pop-Up Book of Phobias* as well as *The Pop-Up Book of Nightmares* and *Self-Helpless: The Greatest Self-Help Books You'll Never Read* (with Jonathan Bines).

Jeannie Hayden is an award-winning illustrator and graphic designer whose client list includes Nickelodeon and the American Museum of Natural History. She is also an accomplished fine artist. You can find her oil paintings at jeanniehayden.com.